# TAPESTRY

## GLOBAL VIEWS

*Reading about World Issues*

# TAPESTRY

The **Tapestry** program of language
materials is based on the concepts
presented in ***The Tapestry Of
Language Learning:*** *The Individual
in the Communicative Classroom* by
Robin C. Scarcella &
Rebecca L. Oxford.

❖

Each title in this program focuses on:

❖

Individual learner strategies and
instruction

❖

The relatedness of skills

❖

Ongoing self-assessment

❖

Authentic material as input

❖

Theme-based learning linked to task-
based instruction

❖

Attention to all aspects of
communicative competence

# TAPESTRY

# GLOBAL VIEWS

## *Reading about World Issues*

M. E. Sokolik

Heinle & Heinle Publishers
A Division of Wadsworth, Inc.
Boston, Massachusetts, 02116, USA

The publication of *Global Views* was directed by the members of the Heinle & Heinle ESL Publishing Team:

David Lee, Editorial Director
Susan Mraz, Marketing Manager
Lisa McLaughlin, Production Editor

Also participating in the publication of this program were:

Publisher:  Stanley J. Galek
Editorial Production Manager:  Elizabeth Holthaus
Assistant Editor:  Kenneth Mattsson
Manufacturing Coordinator:  Mary Beth Lynch
Full Service Project Manager/Compositor:  Monotype Composition Company
Interior Design:  Maureen Lauran
Cover Design:  Maureen Lauran

Manufactured in the United States of America.

ISBN: 0-8384-2313-2

Heinle & Heinle Publishers is a division of Wadsworth, Inc.

10 9 8 7 6 5 4 3

*To my intrepid siblings,*
*Katherine and Charles,*
*in no particular order.*

# PHOTO CREDITS

Chapter 1: 1, Nogues/Sygma; 2, Sygma; 3, Kraft/Sygma; 17, AP/WWP; 19, Gedda/Sygma; AP/WWP.

Chapter 2: 23, Keler/Sygma; 27; 29, Okonewski/Image Works; 31, Topham/Image Works; 34, Topham/Image Works; 41, AP/WWP.

Chapter 3: 43, Hudson/Sygma; 46, Laffont/Sygma; 49, John Elk, III; 51, Sygma; 58, Richard B. Levine; 63, Frank Oberle, Jr./Photo Resources; 64, Ulrike Welsch.

Chapter 4: 67, Langevin/Sygma; 68, Sygma; 74, Matthew Brady/AP/WWP; Ralpho/Photo Researchers; 75, Underwood Photo Archives; 77 Sygma; 82, Goldberg/Sygma.

Chapter 5: 87, Applewhite/AP/WWP; 91, Tracy/Photo Resources; 94 Breummer/Peter Arnold; 97, Cantor/AP/WWP; 98 JohnElk, III; 102, Villafuerk/AP/WWP.

Chapter 6: 105 & 116, Zimberg/Sygma; 106, IPA/Peter Arnold; 110, Jarecke/Contact Press Images; 113 Carini/Image Works; 120, Fournier/Contact Press Images; Tom Tracy/Photo Resources;121, Crandell/Image Works.

Chapter 7: 123, NASA/Peter Arnold; 126 Shooting Star International/Universal; 130, Sygma; 133, Helber/AP/WWP; 137, (left) NASA/Sygma, (right) Foto Khronika/TASS/Sovfoto.

Chapter 8: 139, Carlos Humberto/Contact Press Images; 140 Mangino/Image Works; 142, Wells/Image Works; 145, Frances M. Roberts; 146, V. Musaelyan/TASS/Sovfoto; 148, O'Rourke/Image Works; 150, Brack/Black Star.

Chapter 9: 155, Martha Cooper/Peter Arnold; 157, Topham/Image Works; 159, Wells/Image Works; 160, Richard B. Levine; 163, Thomas Laird; 165, Waugh/Peter Arnold; 168, Sound/Contact Press Images; Topham/Image Works.

Chapter 10: 177, Scala/Art Resources; 178, Cranitsas/Image Works; 179, Burbank/Image Works; 191, Bob Daemmrich/Image Works; 193, Shooting Star International; 194, Tanaka/Blaney Picture Cube.

# MAPS

Gayle Hayes

# ACKNOWLEDGMENTS

"The Chance that Will Not Return," © Feb. 26, 1990, *U.S. News and World Report.*

"Good-Bye SWA, Welcome Namibia," printed with permission by South Africa Communication Service.

"Growing Up," Copyright © 1991 by *Harper's Magazine.* All rights reserved. Reprinted from the October issue by special permission.

"Third World USA," printed with permission of *New Perspectives Quarterly.*

"New World" by Jonathon Raban reprinted by permission of Aitken & Stone, Ltd., London.

"Lost Sister," reprinted from *Picture Bride* by Cathy Song, reprinted by permission of the author and Yale University Press. © 1983 Yale University Press.

"Saving the Family Farm," printed with permission of *Food First News.*

"Napa, California," from *Women Are Not Roses.* Copyright © by Ana Castillo 1984. Originally published by Arte Publico Press. Reprinted by permission of Susan Bergholz Literary Services, New York.

"One Teen's Bout with Hunger," from *Scholastic Update,* January 27, 1989. Copyright © 1989 by Scholastic, Inc. Reprinted by permission of the publisher.

"Helping Africa End Its Famine," printed with permission by *World Press Review.*

"Anatomy of a Cheeseburger," from *Beyond Beef* by Jeremy Rifkin. Copyright © 1992 by Jeremy Rifkin. Used by permission of the publisher, Dutton, an imprint of New American Library, a division of Penguin Books USA, Inc.

"Hamburger Diplomacy," printed with permission by *Soviet Life Magazine.*

"Eye for an Eye," "Beirut Diary," "The Man from Hiroshima," "The State of Europe," "Christmas Eve, 1989," and "Craigavon Bridge" are all reprinted by permission of *Granta.*

Grass. © Carl Sandburg Family Trust, Frank Parker & M. Greenbaum, Trustees.

"I Was Far from Confident," © 1991, *Time* Inc. Reprinted by permission.

Newsweek "America At War" Advertisement, from *Newsweek* 1991. All Rights Reserved. Reprinted by permission.

"Paradise Lost: The Ravaged Rain Forest," reprinted with permission from *Multinational Monitor,* PO Box 19405 Washington, DC 20036. Individual subscription $25/year.

"Saving the Planet" reprinted by permission from *The Progressive,* 409 East Main St., Madison, WI 53703.

"Fire and Ice," from *The Poetry of Robert Frost,* edited by Edward Connery Lathem. Copyright © 1923, © 1969 by Holt, Rinehart and Winston. Copyright 1951 by Robert Frost. Reprinted by permission of Henry Holt and Co., Inc.

"Watching the Rain in Galicia," Copyright © 1991 Gabriel García Marquez.

"A Small Place," excerpt from *A Small Place* by Jamaica Kincaid. Copyright © 1988 by Jamaica Kincaid. Reprinted by permission of Farrar, Straus and Giroux, Inc.

"Observations after Landfall," from *The Journal of Christopher Columbus* translated by Cecile Jane. Copyright © 1960 by Clarkson N. Potter, Inc. Reprinted by permission of Clarkson N. Potter, Inc., a division of Crown Publishers, Inc.

"Events in the Skies," © 1987 Doris Lessing. Reprinted by permission of Jonathan Clowes, Ltd., London, on behalf of Doris Lessing.

"The Death of the Night," reprinted by permission of the author.

"Star-Swirls," from *The Beginning and the End* by Robinson Jeffers. Copyright © 1963 by Garth Jeffers and Donnan Jeffers. Reprinted by permission of Random House, Inc.

"Manned Space Flight Controversy" printed with permission of the *Houston Chronicle.*

Year 2010 advertisement, printed with permission of Computeach.

"Psst! Wanna Buy a Spaceship?" Reprinted by permission of *Omni,* © 1991, Omni Publications International, Ltd.

"How Media Literacy Can Change the Word," reprinted with permission of the *Independent Film and Video Monthly,* a publication of the New York City based association of Independent Video Filmmakers and the authors.

CompuServe advertisement, printed with permission of Compuserve Incorporated.

"The Shrinking World of Totalitarian TV," reprinted with permission from *Broadcasting* magazine, September 10, 1990, © 1990 by Cahners Publishing Company.

"Watch Local, See Global," printed with permission by *Z Magazine.* 150 W. Canton, Boston, MA 02116.

"Ohiyesa," reprinted from *Touch the Earth.* Copyright © 1971 by T.C. McLuhan. Paperback edition originally published by Outerbridge & Dienstfrey, NY 1971; Simon and Schuster 1972. Reprinted with permission of Loretta Barrett Books, New York and the author.

"Pashu Lama: Meditation and Manacles," reprinted from *Whole Earth Review,* No. 72, Fall 1991; subscriptions to WER are $20 a year (4 issues) from PO Box 38, Sausalito, CA 94966, (415) 332-1716.

"Iron and Silk," from *Iron and Silk* by Mark Salzman. Copyright © 1986 by Mark Salzman. Reprinted by permission of Random House, Inc.

Seventeen Syllables from *Seventeen Syllables.* Copyright © 1988 by Hisaye Yamamoto. Used with permission of the author and Kitchen Table: Women of Color Press, P.O. Box 908, Latham, NY 12110.

"You Are What You Say," reprinted with permission of Robin Lakoff.

# WELCOME TO TAPESTRY

*E*nter the world of Tapestry! Language learning can be seen as an ever-developing tapestry woven with many threads and colors. The elements of the tapestry are related to different language skills like listening and speaking, reading and writing; the characteristics of the teachers; the desires, needs, and backgrounds of the students; and the general second language development process. When all these elements are working together harmoniously, the result is a colorful, continuously growing tapestry of language competence of which the student and the teacher can be proud.

This volume is part of the Tapestry program for students of English as a second language (ESL) at levels from beginning to "bridge" (which follows the advanced level and prepares students to enter regular postsecondary programs along with native English speakers). Tapestry levels include:

Beginning
Low Intermediate
High Intermediate
Low Advanced
High Advanced
Bridge

Because the Tapestry Program provides a unified theoretical and pedagogical foundation for all its components, you can optimally use all the Tapestry student books in a coordinated fashion as an entire curriculum of materials. (They will be published from 1993 to 1995 with further editions likely thereafter.) Alternatively, you can decide to use just certain Tapestry volumes, depending on your specific needs.

Tapestry is primarily designed for ESL students at postsecondary institutions in North America. Some want to learn ESL for academic or career advancement, others for social and personal reasons. Tapestry builds directly on all these motivations. Tapestry stimulates learners to do their best. It enables learners to use English naturally and to develop fluency as well as accuracy.

## Tapestry Principles

The following principles underlie the instruction provided in all of the components of the Tapestry program.

### EMPOWERING LEARNERS

Language learners in Tapestry classrooms are active and increasingly responsible for developing their English language skills and related cultural abilities. This self-direction leads to better, more rapid learning. Some cultures virtually train their students to be passive in the classroom, but Tapestry weans them from passivity by providing exceptionally high-interest materials, colorful and motivating activities, personalized self-reflection tasks, peer tutoring and other forms of cooperative learning, and powerful learning strategies to boost self-direction in learning.

The empowerment of learners creates refreshing new roles for teachers, too. The teacher serves as facilitator, co-communicator, diagnostician, guide, and helper. Teachers are set free to be more creative at the same time their students become more autonomous learners.

### HELPING STUDENTS IMPROVE THEIR LEARNING STRATEGIES

Learning strategies are the behaviors or steps an individual uses to enhance his or her learning. Examples are taking notes, practicing, finding a conversation partner, analyzing words, using background knowledge, and controlling anxiety. Hundreds of such strategies have been identified. Successful language learners use language learning strategies that are most effective for them given their particular learning style, and they put them together smoothly to fit the needs of a given language task. On the other hand, the learning strategies of less successful learners are a desperate grab-bag of ill-matched techniques.

All learners need to know a wide range of learning strategies. All learners need systematic practice in choosing and applying strategies that are relevant for various learning needs. Tapestry is one of the only ESL programs that overtly weaves a comprehensive set of learning strategies into language activities in all its volumes. These learning strategies are arranged in six broad categories throughout the Tapestry books:

Forming concepts
Personalizing
Remembering new material
Managing your learning
Understanding and using emotions
Overcoming limitations

The most useful strategies are sometimes repeated and flagged with a note, "It Works! Learning Strategy . . ." to remind students to use a learning strategy they have already encountered. This recycling reinforces the value of learning strategies and provides greater practice.

### RECOGNIZING AND HANDLING LEARNING STYLES EFFECTIVELY

Learners have different learning styles (for instance, visual, auditory, hands-on; reflective, impulsive; analytic, global; extroverted, introverted; closure-oriented, open). Particularly in an ESL setting, where students come from vastly different cultural backgrounds, learning styles differences abound and can cause "style conflicts."

Unlike most language instruction materials, Tapestry provides exciting activities specifically tailored to the needs of students with a large range of learning styles. You can use any Tapestry volume with the confidence that the activities and materials are intentionally geared for many different styles. Insights from the latest educational and psychological research undergird this style-nourishing variety.

## OFFERING AUTHENTIC, MEANINGFUL COMMUNICATION

Students need to encounter language that provides authentic, meaningful communication. They must be involved in real-life communication tasks that cause them to *want* and *need* to read, write, speak, and listen to English. Moreover, the tasks—to be most effective—must be arranged around themes relevant to learners.

Themes like family relationships, survival in the educational system, personal health, friendships in a new country, political changes, and protection of the environment are all valuable to ESL learners. Tapestry focuses on topics like these. In every Tapestry volume, you will see specific content drawn from very broad areas such as home life, science and technology, business, humanities, social sciences, global issues, and multiculturalism. All the themes are real and important, and they are fashioned into language tasks that students enjoy.

At the advanced level, Tapestry also includes special books each focused on a single broad theme. For instance, there are two books on business English, two on English for science and technology, and two on academic communication and study skills.

## UNDERSTANDING AND VALUING DIFFERENT CULTURES

Many ESL books and programs focus completely on the "new" culture, that is, the culture which the students are entering. The implicit message is that ESL students should just learn about this target culture, and there is no need to understand their own culture better or to find out about the cultures of their international classmates. To some ESL students, this makes them feel their own culture is not valued in the new country.

Tapestry is designed to provide a clear and understandable entry into North American culture. Nevertheless, the Tapestry Program values *all* the cultures found in the ESL classroom. Tapestry students have constant opportunities to become "culturally fluent" in North American culture while they are learning English, but they also have the chance to think about the cultures of their classmates and even understand their home culture from different perspectives.

## INTEGRATING THE LANGUAGE SKILLS

Communication in a language is not restricted to one skill or another. ESL students are typically expected to learn (to a greater or lesser degree) all four language skills: reading, writing, speaking, and listening. They are also expected to develop strong grammatical competence, as well as becoming socioculturally sensitive and knowing what to do when they encounter a "language barrier."

Research shows that multi-skill learning is more effective than isolated-skill learning, because related activities in several skills provide reinforcement and refresh the learner's memory. Therefore, Tapestry integrates all the skills. A given Tapestry volume might highlight one skill, such as reading, but all other skills are also included to support and strengthen overall language development.

However, many intensive ESL programs are divided into classes labeled according to one skill (Reading Comprehension Class) or at most two skills (Listening/Speaking Class or Oral Communication Class). The volumes in the Tapestry Program can easily be used to fit this traditional format, because each volume clearly identifies its highlighted or central skill(s).

Grammar is interwoven into all Tapestry volumes. However, there is also a separate reference book for students, *The Tapestry Grammar,* and a Grammar Strand composed of grammar "work-out" books at each of the levels in the Tapestry Program.

## Other Features of the Tapestry Program

### PILOT SITES

It is not enough to provide volumes full of appealing tasks and beautiful pictures. Users deserve to know that the materials have been pilot-tested. In many ESL series, pilot testing takes place at only a few sites or even just in the classroom of the author. In contrast, Heine & Heinle Publishers have developed a network of Tapestry Pilot Test Sites throughout North America. At this time, there are approximately 40 such sites, although the number grows weekly. These sites try out the materials and provide suggestions for revisions. They are all actively engaged in making Tapestry the best program possible.

### AN OVERALL GUIDEBOOK

To offer coherence to the entire Tapestry Program and especially to offer support for teachers who want to understand the principles and practice of Tapestry, we have written a book entitled, *The Tapestry of Language Learning: The Individual in the Communicative Classroom* (Scarcella and Oxford, published in 1992 by Heinle & Heinle).

## A Last Word

We are pleased to welcome you to Tapestry! We use the Tapestry principles every day, and we hope these principles—and all the books in the Tapestry Program—provide you the same strength, confidence, and joy that they give us. We look forward to comments from both teachers and students who use any part of the Tapestry Program.

Rebecca L. Oxford
University of Alabama
Tuscaloosa, Alabama

Robin C. Scarcella
University of California at Irvine
Irvine, California

# PREFACE

*B*eing a good reader is not only a matter of reading *fast.* Good readers understand what they read, and most of all, *enjoy* their reading.

This book will present strategies that can help you to become a more effective reader. Some of the strategies described may work for you, some may not—trying them will help you decide which work best for you.

Here are some overall strategies to practice as you work with this book.

## DICTIONARY USE

Dictionaries are a wonderful tool to aid understanding. Both bilingual dictionaries and English-English dictionaries can help you better comprehend what you read. However, relying on a dictionary while you are reading can slow you down, and interrupt the ideas being presented in the reading. This can actually cause you to understand *less* of what you read, not more! A good strategy is to try to read the entire reading before you look words up. Instead, use a highlighting marker or pencil to mark the words you don't understand. After you finish reading, look back at your marked words. Were you able to determine the meaning of the word without looking it up? Sometimes the reading gives you enough information that you don't have to look it up. If you still need to look it up, you may make notes on the definition in Appendix C provided at the end of the text. Using the word in a sentence may help you to understand it better.

## READ ON YOUR OWN

Reading well is also a matter of practice. Read as often as you can, and read a variety of materials. Read magazines and newspapers. Even reading the back of a breakfast cereal box will help? When you are feeling more comfortable with your reading, challenge yourself by reading a novel. You'll find a list of novels recommended for ESL students in Appendix B of this book.

## KEEP A JOURNAL

It will help you to keep records of the strategies you try. Make notes for yourself describing the strategy you used, and whether you felt it helped your reading. Use strategies that work for you again and again.

## TIME YOUR READING

Although understanding of reading is the most important skill in most instances, there are many cases where you want to increase your speed. At the beginnings and ends of some readings you will find spaces to record and calculate your reading speed. You can also record your speeds in Appendix A at the end of the book. There are also several exercises in the text to help you improve your reading speed.

Remember that you reading speed will vary depending on a number of factors, such as:

- purpose of reading
- familiarity with the subject matter
- difficulty of material
- type of reading (for example, newspaper article, poem, etc.)

Throughout the book you will have the opportunity to learn ways to improve your reading speed and to keep track of your progress.

## DEVELOP YOUR OWN STRATEGIES

As you become more aware of strategies and how they can be used, you may notice that you have some strategies that are not mentioned in this book. Make notes of these in your journal, and think about how they work for you.

## The Structure of this Book

In addition to the strategies, each chapter presents several features to help integrate reading into your learning experience.

- Planning & Goals: This section gives you the opportunity to think about what you want to accomplish while you complete that chapter.
- "Looking Ahead" encourages you to think about the readings that will be presented in each chapter, and presents questions for you to consider before you read.
- Each chapter includes a listening exercise that can help you understand more about the topic of the chapter. You are encouraged to do the listening exercise in order to broaden your knowledge about the information presented in the chapter.
- The readings in each chapter are preceded by a prereading question or activity. These activities will help you to activate and strengthen your knowledge about the material in the reading.

Each reading is followed by different types of questions:

- Comprehension: Comprehension questions to help you remember what you read.
- Analysis: Different types of questions asking you to analyze either the language or the ideas of the reading.
- Timed Readings: Some readings give you spaces to record your reading speed.
- Footnotes and statistics are provided to give you more information about the readings, or about difficult vocabulary items.
- Summary Exercises: At the end of each chapter, there are activities to help you synthesize the ideas presented in the chapter.
- Themes: Four sections—Discuss, Debate, Role-play, and Write—present topics for discussion and writing.
- The Cultural Dimension: This section encourages you to go out into your community and talk about ideas and opinions.
- Evaluation: Each chapter gives you an opportunity to evaluate your own performance by asking you to think about what you learned.

## Acknowledgments

I firmly believe that the first to be acknowledged in any textbook should be the students—those students who participated in the development and piloting of a work, as well as those students who put themselves trustingly into the hands of teachers and textbooks every day. I hope this project lives up to their expectations.

I would then like to thank David Lee for approaching me with this project. His confidence in my work as well as his insights into the field have helped shape this book as much as anything. Ken Mattsson also deserves high praise for his assistance and encouragement.

In addition, I would like to recognize Robin Scarcella and Rebecca Oxford for their suggestions and support, and for their championing of this series. Their guidance has made this jump into unknown waters easier.

Gary James, through sharing his ideas and his manuscript for another volume of this series, has also been of tremendous help, by example.Thanks also to Gaye Childress (University of North Texas), Marianne Reynolds (Mercer County Community College), and Judith Cook (American University) for their comments during the development of this book.

To those who assisted through piloting parts of this work, Katherine Watson and Colleen Hildebrand (University of California, Irvine), Scott Schiefelbein (Ohio University), and Eleanor K. Wilborn (California State University, Los Angeles) I would like to extend a special thank you.

Finally, and as always, I would like to thank my husband and partner, Michael Smith, whose encouragement and support makes anything possible, even probable.

M. E. Sokolik
University of California
Berkeley, California

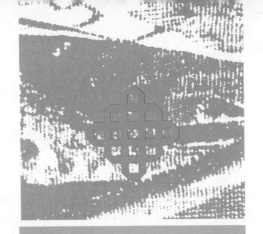

# CONTENTS

# *Changing Political Systems*

**Managing Your Learning: Setting goals for yourself helps you improve areas that are important to you.**

Use the table below to help identify the reading skills you wish to improve. Your goals may change from chapter to chapter.

List in order of priority (with 1 as 'most important') the goals that are important to you.

| GOAL | RANK |
|---|---|
| **A.** To increase reading speed | ____ |
| **B.** To increase comprehension of main ideas | ____ |
| **C.** To improve vocabulary understanding | ____ |
| **D.** To learn more about the information in this chapter | ____ |
| **E.** To improve understanding of style and grammar | ____ |

## LOOKING AHEAD

The world is always changing, but recent history shows this is truer than ever. While some countries try to join together and form new alliances, others split apart over age-old tensions. Makers of world maps have had a lot of work to do redrawing the boundaries of Germany, the U.S.S.R., Yugoslavia, and southern Africa, among others.

This chapter looks at some of the recent changes in the world political order. Here are the titles of the readings found in this chapter:

"The State of Europe: Christmas Eve, 1989" by Stephen Spender

"The Chance that Will Not Return" by Vaclav Havel

"Good-bye to Berlin" by Ian Walker

"Good-bye SWA, Welcome Namibia," by Gert Coetzee

"Growing Up," by Richard Afari Baafour

## LEARNING STRATEGY

**Forming Concepts: Relying on what you already know improves
your reading comprehension.**

Think about the titles of the readings above. What can you guess about the
contents of this chapter? Use the questions below to help you.

1. What kinds of topics (specifically) would you guess will be covered in this
   chapter?
2. Which titles are "mysterious" to you? Why?
3. Are there any authors whose names are familiar to you? What do you know
   about them?
4. Look ahead at the graphic material included in this chapter. What does it
   tell you about the subject matter?
5. What would you like to know about this topic? Write two or three questions you have about the world's changing political structures.

## Try a New Strategy

Identifying your own goals will help you to determine what is important to *you*.
Make a list of at least ten things you would like to improve in your reading. (For
example, would you like to understand magazines better?) Keep your list and
refer to it occasionally. Add new goals to it as they develop.

## LEARNING STRATEGY

**Forming Concepts: Learning more about a topic through listening
helps you prepare for new ideas and vocabulary.**

### LISTENING

Watch a national television news program
on ABC, CBS, NBC, or CNN, then answer the
questions in section A. In class, find a classmate
who watched a different program, and
complete the questions in section B.

**Remembering New Material: Taking notes helps you recall important details.**

**A.** On your own, use the following spaces to take notes as you watch the news broadcast.

1. The name of the television network I watched was _____

_____

2. The name of the main newscaster on the program was _____

_____

3. Describe the major news story of the day (the major story is typically the one told first in the broadcast). _____

_____

_____

4. How many stories were devoted to international topics?_____

5. Describe two other news stories that were reported on the program.

_____

_____

_____

_____

## Threads

Nobel Peace Prize Winners—
1991 Aung San Suu Kyi
1990 Mikhael Gorbachov
1989 Dalai Lama
1988 U.N. Peacekeeping Forces
1987 Oscar Arias Sánchez

**Forming Concepts: Asking someone to repeat or rephrase helps you understand better.**

**B.** With a partner:
1. Describe to your partner your answer for question 3 above. Try to recall as many details as possible.
2. Compare your answers for question 4. Were they approximately the same number, or were they different? Ask your partner the following question: Do you think the news in your own country covers more or less international news than the U.S. news broadcast you watched?
3. Describe your answer to question 5 to your partner. Explain which story you found most interesting, and why.

## ANALYSIS

Look at the cartoon carefully.

1. What is the difference between the two maps?
2. What recent events are portrayed by this political cartoon?

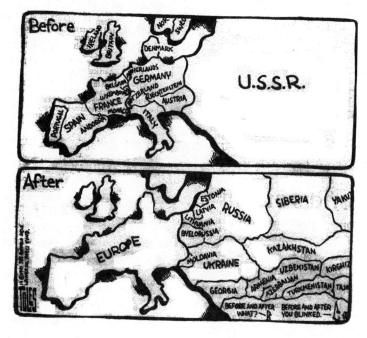

Drawing by Toles; © 1991
Universal Press Syndicate.

---

### LEARNING STRATEGY

**Managing Your Learning: Making lists of relevant vocabulary lets you prepare for new reading material.**

## PREREADING ACTIVITY

With a partner, list all of the Eastern or Central European countries you can think of. What difficulties did you have in compiling this list?

## THE STATE OF EUROPE, CHRISTMAS EVE, 1989

*Stephen Spender*

1  Perhaps because I am eighty what is happening today in the Soviet Union, East Germany, Czechoslovakia, Hungary and Bulgaria has the effect of making me feel that I am witnessing apocalyptic° events out of the Book of Revelations.[1] I do not apologize for beginning on this personal note. For the collapse of the totalitarian regimes° in the Soviet Union and Eastern Europe is something that I had given up hope of witnessing in my lifetime. I was sure that it would happen eventually but that it would be perpetually postponed to the next century, after the millennium. I now have the almost Biblical sense of being privileged to
2  witness a miracle.

Perhaps some young people have the same kind of feeling. A historic event may seem to contemporaries° part of a larger impersonal history being unfolded

*apocalyptic events are occurrences that are predicted by "divine inspiration"*

*governments*

*people of the same generation, peers*

5

before their eyes, and yet at the same time strike each separately as being his or her intensely felt personal experience. The assassination of President Kennedy[2] had this effect on thousands of people who, notoriously almost, remember what they were doing at the moment when they heard the news of Kennedy's death.

[1] "The Book of Revelations" is the final chapter of the New Testament of the Christian Bible. In this chapter, Jesus reveals the future of the world to St. John the Divine.

[2] John F. Kennedy was the 35th President of the United States. He was shot November 22, 1963 in Dallas, Texas by Lee Harvey Oswald. His assassination is, however, the subject of controversy, and there are other theories about his death. The 1991 film *JFK* deals with an alternative conspiracy theory.

Source: Excerpted from "The State of Europe: Christmas Eve, 1989" *Granta* 30, 1990, p. 168.

## LEARNING STRATEGY

**Remembering New Material: Trying to remember what you understand from a reading helps you develop better comprehension skills.**

## COMPREHENSION

Answer these questions without looking back at the reading.

1. How old is Mr. Spender?
   **a.** 50   **b.** 60   **c.** 70   **d.** 80
2. What event is he discussing?
   **a.** the Bible   **b.** the changes in Eastern Europe
   **c.** the Kennedy Assassination   **d.** the new millennium
3. What emotion does he display in this writing?
   **a.** annoyance   **b.** unhappiness
   **c.** excitement   **d.** skepticism

## LEARNING STRATEGY

**Managing Your Learning: Working with classmates helps you develop your language skills.**

## ANALYSIS

The author of this story says: "A historic event may seem to contemporaries part of a larger impersonal history being unfolded before their eyes, and yet at the same time strike each separately as being his or her intensely felt personal experience."

What do you think he means?

With a small group of your classmates, choose one important event in the news that affected you personally. Prepare a group report in which each of you provides the following information:

**a.** Give a short description of event and the date it occurred.

**b.** What were you doing the moment you heard the news?

_____

_____

**c.** Why was this event important to you?

_____

_____

**d.** Describe how the news made you feel.

_____

_____

**e.** Explain how the news affected you or your family personally.

_____

_____

Compile your answers and choose one group member to make an oral report to the class.

### LEARNING STRATEGY

**Forming Concepts: Sometimes it may help to concentrate on grammar so you can understand unfamiliar constructions.**

Examine the following quotations. You may find their structures and/or vocabulary difficult. Rephrase each of the sentences into a simpler sentence. Then explain why you think the author chose the more complicated wording. Obviously, many different answers are possible. Compare your responses with a classmate's in order to see another possibility.

**a.** ". . .what is happening today in the Soviet Union, East Germany, Czechoslovakia, Hungary and Bulgaria has the effect of making me feel that I am witnessing apocalyptic events out of the Book of Revelations."

_____

_____

**b.** ". . .the collapse of the totalitarian regimes in the Soviet Union and Eastern Europe is something that I had given up hope of witnessing in my lifetime."

_____

_____

What is the man at the table doing? Why?

*Drawing by Lorenz, © 1989 The New Yorker Magazine, Inc.*

*LEARNING STRATEGY*

**Forming Concepts: Understanding the main idea helps you comprehend the entire reading.**

## Prereading Question

Read the first paragraph of this reading. What do you think the rest of the reading will be about?

### THE CHANCE THAT WILL NOT RETURN

*Vaclav Havel*

1   What kind of place could or should the new Europe be? What principles would hold this community together and what could it contribute to the rest of the world?

2   The spirit of history moves in mysterious ways, and it is hardly possible to pose a definite answer to these questions. But perhaps it is possible to glimpse in the mist of the unknown an outline of the place that Europe could become.

First of all, because Europe is as much an idea as a place, it would have to remain bigger than a sum of its parts. Any concept of a new Europe will have to deal with the existence of the United States and the Soviet Union, and not only for political reasons.

3   The United States, though completely outside Europe, is not entirely non-European. It was born out of Europe in a rebellion against it. The Soviet Union, though not completely inside Europe, has gravitated toward Europe for centuries, without ever taking the final step. In this century, the U.S. and the Soviet Union fought a war against a totalitarian ideology that threatened to undermine the very idea of Europe. Then, they almost fought each other over another incarnation of totalitarianism. If that had happened, the battlefield almost certainly would have been Europe once again. Thus, both the Americans and the Russians, though in different degrees, may lay claims on the loyalty of Europeans. And both, fighting as they have for control of the continent, have earned different measures of distrust from Europeans.

4   If Europe becomes whole, it will have no need for guardians or protectors. But there should always be a place in Europe for the United States, the strongest democracy in the world. And there should be a place in Europe for a truly

democratic Soviet Union. The histories and destinies of Europeans, Russians, and Americans are interlinked in countless ways.

Source: US News and World Report, February 26, 1990.

**Remembering New Material: Review the purpose and tone of a reading passage so you can remember more effectively.**

## COMPREHENSION

Answer these questions without referring to the reading.

1. Havel's main purpose in this writing is:
   **a.** to discuss a foreign relations policy for Europe, the U.S., and the U.S.S.R.;
   **b.** to explain the interrelationships between Europe, the U.S., and the U.S.S.R.;
   **c.** to define the consequences of World War II, and the loyalties of Europe;
   **d.** to explore the possible future philosophy of a united Europe.
2. Havel's overall tone is
   **a.** diplomatic  **b.** pessimistic  **c.** argumentative  **d.** philosophical

## ANALYSIS

1. Underline two passages that you found difficult to understand when you first read the passage. Rephrase those passages:

   line numbers: _____      Rephrasing:_____

   _____

   _____

   line numbers: _____      Rephrasing:_____

   _____

   _____

2. Locate a phrase that shows that Havel is a writer as well as a political leader.

   line numbers: _____      Rephrasing:_____

   _____

   _____

3. Compare this reading with the first one in this chapter. What important vocabulary items are shared by both articles? Make a list of them here.

   _____

   _____

Compare your responses with those of a classmate, and discuss your choices.

**Remembering New Material: Picturing scenes in your mind helps you remember and understand your reading.**

 As you read the following passage, stop every time you see a star (☆) in the margin, and try to imagine what the scene looks like. You can even create a drawing of it, if you feel it might help.

## GOOD-BYE TO BERLIN

*Ian Walker*

1    I'm in the cafe beneath Savigny Platz S-Bahn train station in Berlin wondering in which order to consume my Camembert°, ham, raspberry jam, French bread, butter, one strawberry, a slice of kiwi fruit, and a banana. The mournful sax of Stan Getz[1] dribbles from the speakers. It's four in the afternoon.

*type of soft French cheese*

2    I am, you see, coming to terms with the death of one particular kind of city, one I knew well, and the birth of another, whose personality will remain a mystery for a while. I've been back in the city six days talking to different people I know. All they have in common is that the pattern of their lives has been broken. My best friend in East Berlin, a member of the Communist Party, is exhilarated at the prospect of starting his own architectural practice. An Englishwoman who has lived in East Berlin since 1949 now says if she has to live under capitalism she would prefer to do so in her own country. Turkish guest workers in Kreuzberg, the ghetto by the wall in the American sector, are worried that they may lose their jobs (why employ a Turk when an East German comes just as cheap?) and be sent home on the train to Istanbul.

3    I still feel shell-shocked, even after six days. All I can do is sit here watching the trains go by, away from the newly overcrowded streets and shops. The whole city is in motion. The Moscow-via-Warsaw express brings 5,000 a day into West Berlin, mostly poor people who try to sell their few possessions for deutsche marks in the junk markets that have sprung up on the muddy ground near Potsdamer Platz. The population of Berlin is expected to grow rapidly from four million to six million. The money is moving quickly too. Volkswagen, Opel, and German Ford are building new headquarters in Berlin. Property developers are moving on East Berlin. There are fortunes to be made, but not by the Polish peasants selling turnips and coats in the streets.

4    I can understand why many of West Berlin's artists and intellectuals feel like their party has been invaded by thousands of gate-crashers who drank all the booze and changed the music. The question is: where to go?

5    New York is widely proposed. Good and dirty, people say, but a nightmare finding an apartment unless you're prepared to live way out in Brooklyn or even New Jersey. Prague has its adherents, as does Budapest. Barcelona is a possibility, though they say Valencia is quite funky° and much cheaper. One of my friends, a scientist working in computer art, is packing his bags for Zurich. He thinks Berlin will become the Disneyland and Las Vegas of Central Europe, a city of folkloric theme-parks and meretricious° entertainment. He sees no place for art in the new Berlin boomtown.

*artistic, modern*

*attractive, but not of high quality*

6    So what do I think? I'm listening to an American voice speaking loudly in English to Germans, and I'm wondering how much longer Germans will acquiesce in the Anglo-American cultural occupation of their country.

7    Looking back, sipping my espresso, I think about how I was originally drawn here by the glamour of Berlin that all began with Marlene Dietrich.[2] The death of Berlin's glamour was celebrated last November, which was probably why I had to come back. I'd written a book about this city that had suddenly become history overnight.

[1]Saxophone player, born 1927, died 1991. Getz was recognized as a great player and an innovator of "cool jazz," which dominated the music scene in the late 1940s and early 1950s.

[2]Born 1904 in Germany, a singer and actress of world renown. Her most famous films include *The Blue Angel* and *Sign of the Cross.* She died in May of 1992.

Source: 20/20, June 1990, as it appeared in *Utne Reader* No. 41, Sept./Oct. 1990, pp. 113-114.

## LEARNING STRATEGY

**Remembering New Material: Reviewing key ideas and details lets you remember.**

## COMPREHENSION

Answer these questions without looking back at the reading passage.

1. The main idea in this passage is:
   a. American influence in Germany;
   b. the changes in Berlin;
   c. the problems with guest workers in Germany;
   d. the life of artists in Berlin.
2. How long has the author been in Berlin?
   a. six years
   b. six months
   c. six days
   d. six hours
3. Why is the population of Berlin expected to grow?
   a. Millions of immigrants will come from Eastern Europe;
   b. Thousands of artists will come from Zurich and New York;
   c. There will be a new Disneyland there;
   d. There will be many bargains to be found in the shops.

## ANALYSIS

Good-Bye to Berlin involves several words and phrases that are slang or colloquial. What do these words mean? Complete the following sentences to show you understand their meanings. Compare your answers with a classmate. Make corrections if you discover you misunderstood the meaning of any of the words.

**a.** If you were *shell-shocked,* you would probably _____

_____

**b.** A *gate-crasher* usually _____

_____

**c.** If you had too much *booze* you would probably _____

_____

**d.** A *funky* neighborhood would probably have_____

_____

*LEARNING STRATEGY*

**Forming Concepts: Expanding your vocabulary and grammar helps you increase your reading speed and comprehension.**

## STRUCTURE

**A.** Look at the following sentences, taken from the reading. With a small group of your classmates, discuss the questions that follow each one.
  **1.** "I am, you see, coming to terms with the death of one particular kind of city, one I knew well, and the birth of another, whose personality will remain a mystery for a while."
  What does the author mean in this sentence? Which city is dying? Which is being born?
  **2.** "I can understand why many of West Berlin's artists and intellectuals feel like their party has been invaded by thousands of gate-crashers who drank all the booze and changed the music."
  What do you think this sentence means? Why did the author use this image?
  **3.** Identify any other passage you found difficult. Discuss the possible meaning with your group.
**B.** Now, on your own, reread the story. Did the discussion of these passages help improve your understanding?

## Prereading exercise

Look at the map of Africa on page 13. Locate the country of Namibia. Also, try to find a picture of the Namibian flag, which is described in this reading.

# GOOD-BYE SWA, WELCOME NAMIBIA

*Gert Coetzee*

No South African in the Windhoek stadium will ever forget the poignant moment of reflection and expectation at thirteen minutes past midnight on March 21, 1990, when the South African flag was lowered for the last time on Namibian soil after seventy years.

After his speech, the South African State President, Mr. F.W. de Klerk, put his hand on his heart and fixed his eyes one last time on the South African flag in the Namibian night-sky. Next to him the Namibian president elect, Mr. Sam Nujoma, also came to attention. Time came to an abrupt standstill. Slowly, jerkily the flag came into motion and unhurriedly made its way downward.

Later, the South African Minister of Foreign Affairs, Mr. R.F. Botha, aptly summarized the spirit of the moment as follows: "The flag was lowered for the last time but, in reality, it rose again in the good neighborliness with Namibia and in the new South Africa which is emerging."

With the last African country of the colonial period gaining independence a chapter was closed, ushering in a new era for the whole South Africa. Once hoisted, Namibia's flag unfurled slowly and, through the lenses of television and other cameras of the some 1000 press representatives, boldly displayed its colors to the world.

A new nation is born! A bright yellow sun in the top left-hand corner of the Namibian flag represents the new sun rising over the African continent. It epitomizes life and energy, Namibia's golden savannahs[2] and the color of the Namib Desert.

The blue, red and green panels are divided by two narrow diagonal white stripes. Blue typifies the clear Namibian sky, the country's precious water resources, the Atlantic Ocean, and the importance of rain. Red embodies Namibia's most important asset, the people, their heroism and their determination to build a future of equal opportunity for all.

White refers to peace and unity, and green to Namibia's vegetation and agricultural resources. Together, the red and white symbolize Namibia's human resources and the green, gold and blue the country's natural resources.

The highlights of the proceedings were the changing of the flags and the inauguration[3] of Sam Nujoma as the Republic of Namibia's first President by the United Nations Secretary-General, Dr. Javier Perez de Quellar.

The festivities lasted a week. Schools had closed four days earlier to enable the nation's youth to take part in the revelry. On Monday and Tuesday, March 19 and 20, airplanes taxied in at Windhoek airport with monotonous regularity. Dignitaries were received by the then president elect, Mr. Sam Nujoma, his entourage and a group of dancing, ululating[4] Namibians.

Sporadic showers did not dampen the activities. Performances by mass choirs, folk dancers, pop groups and singers, gymnasts and

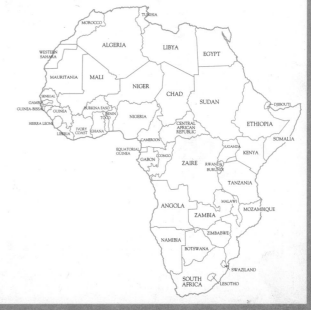

motorcyclists, art programs, an independence march consisting of 75 floats, and matches between Namibia and national sports teams, thrilled the enthusiastic crowds joining in the fun.

Even President Nujoma was rooted to his seat until the end of a rugby match in which Namibia beat Zimbabwe 33-18. All the activities were telecast live by the Namibian Broadcasting Corporation.

However, a tinge of melancholy still remained. The South African Administrator-General of Namibia, Mr. Louis Pienaar, and the UN Special Representative, Mr. Martti Ahtisaari, had to bid their farewells. Their work was finished. The various contingents of Untag, the UN task force, also began their journey home. Only the Kenyan force stayed on as a transitional defense force.

Namibia's independence was the culmination of efforts which had involved South Africa, Namibia, and the international community, especially the UN and its numerous organizations, since the late forties.

The Namibian territory, excluding Walvis Bay and a few islands, was annexed by Germany in 1884. During World War I, South African troops under the command of General Louis Botha occupied the territory as an Allied Power, following the German surrender at Khorab. After the signing of the Treaty of Versailles in 1919 and the establishment of the League of Nations, South Africa was granted guardianship over the then South West Africa.

After World War II, Namibia became the focus of an extremely complex international legal dispute, which eventually also acquired serious political and military dimensions. The first breakthrough in negotiations on the long road to independence came with the adoption of UN Security Council Resolution 435 of 1978. Since then a further series of accords and agreements were concluded.

With the euphoria of the festivities and independence fever a thing of the past, a difficult time lies ahead for the first Namibian government. It will have to put in a great deal of effort to realize its dreams and the promise of freedom. Expectations are

that Namibia's constitution will offer a solution to the problem of participation by all in the political process in a country whose population includes several minority groups.

Two immediate issues to be addressed are education and unemployment, especially after South Africa's withdrawal and suspension of its financial aid for the creation and maintenance of the Namibian infrastructure[4].

In conclusion, President De Klerk's message to the Namibian people: "May God lead you on a road of peace and prosperity. The strife of the past is over. A new mandate for peace is emerging. The sun rises over a new Namibia as part of a new Southern Africa."

[1] Fields.

[2] Official ceremony marking the beginning of an offical's time in government office.

[3] A type of singing.

[4] Roads, bridges, and water and power systems.

Source: Excerpted from *South African Panorama,* May/June 1990, pp. 13-16.

ENDING TIME _____ : _____
TOTAL TIME _____
913 WORDS ÷ _____ MIN = _____ WORDS/MIN

## COMPREHENSION

Without referring to the reading, answer the following questions:

1. Namibia gained independence from which country?
   **a.** Kenya   **b.** Egypt   **c.** Zimbabwe   **d.** South Africa
2. Who will be Namibia's new President?
   **a.** De Klerk   **b.** Nujoma   **c.** Pienaar   **d.** Ahtisaari
3. How might the celebration be described?
   **a.** solemn   **b.** private   **c.** lively   **d.** simple
4. Which country annexed Namibia in the 1800s?
   **a.** Germany   **b.** South Africa   **c.** France   **d.** Zimbabwe
5. What are two important issues that face Namibia? (pick two)
   **a.** education   **b.** religion   **c.** unemployment   **d.** natural resources

## Analysis

### LEARNING STRATEGY

**Forming Concepts: Guessing the meanings of unfamiliar words or phrases lets you use what you already know about English.**

## VOCABULARY

Look at the following phrases taken from the reading. Can you determine the meaning of the underlined word from the surrounding phrase? Write your best guess at its meaning in the space below. Then, compare your answers with a partner's.

1. a *poignant* moment of reflection and expectation

   _____

2. Time came to an *abrupt* standstill.

   _____

3. *ushering in* a new era

   _____

4. once *hoisted*, Namibia's flag *unfurled* slowly

   _____

5. blue *typifies* the clear Namibian sky

   _____

## Threads

On September 17, 1991, the U.N. gave membership to Estonia, Latvia, and Lithuania.

**6.** red *embodies* Namibia's most important asset

_____

**7.** President Nujoma was *rooted to* his seat

_____

**8.** a *tinge* of melancholy still remained

_____

**9.** Namibia's independence was the *culmination* of efforts

_____

**10.** the *euphoria* of the festivities

_____

*LEARNING STRATEGY*

**Managing Your Learning: Taking opportunities to practice what you already know keeps your progress steady.**

Practicing reading aloud may help you to understand the rhythm of language, and the use of words in poetry. Read the following poem to yourself, and then aloud.

### Growing Up

After the politicians
have left with signed copies
of the bilateral agreement
and the assurance of
a constituency for cash
the tycoons will come
it does not matter
at whose invitation
provided someone has
signed off the rationing
and the state of emergency

Tell them we have
anticipated their coming
and our best hospitality
awaits them. . .
We have repealed old laws
if they insist we shall

make new ones, it won't take
more than a stroke of pen
or maybe a gunshot or two
As long as they come
with money and machines
they could count on our goodwill
they could bring along
cash registers the freedom
to count in earnest
and if that suits them
a myth or two to keep up
an image or save a face

but please tell them not to
bother how to profess love
for our people or faith in us
all that old fashioned stuff
for the sincerity of words
doesn't matter any more
since our last economic crisis

*Richard Afari Baafour*

Source: *Harper's Magazine,* October 1991, p 44.

*Mr. Baafour is a civil
servant in the city of
Accra in Ghana.*

## ANALYSIS

Discuss the following questions with a partner or a small group of classmates:

1. The *theme* of a poem refers to its main message, which can usually be stated in one word, such as "poverty" or "love." In one word, what do you think the theme of this poem is? Why did you choose that word?
2. This poem contains very little punctuation. Where would you add punctuation marks? (It may help to read the poem aloud again, to see where the natural pauses come.) Why do you think the author did not include them? What effect does it have on you as a reader?
3. What connection can you see between this poem and the previous article about Namibia?

### LEARNING STRATEGY

**Overcoming Limitations: By choosing a topic you are familiar with, you overcome limitations and communicate more effectively.**

### DISCUSS

Write one question you would like to ask your class concerning the themes presented in this chapter: _____

_____

In a class discussion, ask a classmate your question. Make notes of the questions and answers presented in your class discussion.

### DEBATE

From the class discussion, in a group of four or more students, develop a topic for debate. Then divide your group into two equal parts. Half of your group should argue for one side of the issue you chose, and the other half should argue for the other.

Use the following table to help you develop your arguments.

Topic: _____

State your side's opinion in one sentence:

_____

_____

Reasons you believe this: (State each reason as a sentence).

1. _____
2. _____
3. _____
4. _____

(Use an additional piece of paper if you need more space.) Present your debate to the class. Each side should get the same amount of time to give its arguments.

## ROLE-PLAY

In the reading, "Good-bye to Berlin," you will remember that the author described three friends who were affected by the changes in Germany. Look at the descriptions below of those people.

**a.** The first is a member of the Communist Party from East Berlin, thinking about starting his own architectural practice.
**b.** The second is an Englishwoman who has lived in East Berlin since 1949, considering returning to England.
**c.** The third is a Turkish guest-worker, worried about losing his or her job, and who may be sent home on the train to Istanbul.

In a group with two other classmates, decide which person you would each like to play. Then hold a discussion together about your concerns and hopes for your future.

## WRITE

Below are three phrases adapted from the beginnings of different readings found in this chapter. Choose one of these phrases and write your own remembrance, beginning with that phrase. Change the italicized word to suit your own circumstances (for example, if you chose the first phrase, you would replace "eighty" with your own age.) Refer back to the readings if you need help getting started.

**A.** "Perhaps because I am *eighty* I. . ."
**B.** "I'm in the *café*. . ."
**C.** "No *South African* will ever forget the moment. . ."

Nelson Mandela, at left, spent years in a South African prison because of his opposition to Apartheid. Chinese students, below, faced down tanks during the 1989 protests in Beijing.

## The Cultural Dimension

### LEARNING STRATEGY

**Forming Concepts: Learning more about other cultures helps you understand opinions and facts in your readings.**

1. Interview a classmate about recent changes that have taken place in his or her country. Prepare at least five questions to ask. Report to the class on what you have learned.
2. Interview a U.S. citizen about his or her perspective on the changing world situation. Before your interview, write at least five questions you want to ask. Tape record your interview or take detailed notes. Prepare a written report on your interview.

### LEARNING STRATEGY

**Managing Your Learning: Evaluating what you have learned and how well you are doing can help you focus your learning.**

## Self-Evaluation Questionnaire

Make a list of important new ideas or words you learned from this chapter.

1. _____
2. _____
3. _____
4. _____
5. _____
6. _____
7. _____
8. _____
9. _____
10. _____

## Threads

Lee Teng-hui became the first Taiwanese to become president of the Republic of China on Taiwan in 1988.

You will recall that at the beginning of the chapter, you were asked to determine your goals. Now, review your performance. Look at the vocabulary and comprehension exercises you completed and check your reading speeds. Rate yourself on how you did in each of the following areas for this chapter. Give yourself the following ratings:

**5 excellent   4 good   3 average   2 fair   1 poor**

| | RATING |
|---|---|
| **A.** Improved reading speed | _____ |
| **B.** Understood main ideas | _____ |
| **C.** Increased vocabulary understanding | _____ |
| **D.** Learned more about the topic of the chapter | _____ |
| **E.** Developed more understanding of style and grammar | _____ |

Compare your ratings with the objectives you set at the beginning of this chapter.

# Population and Immigration

*IT WORKS!*
*Learning Strategy:*
*Setting Goals*

As you did in Chapter 1, list in order of priority (with 1 as `most important`) the objectives that are important to you in this chapter.

| GOAL | | RANK |
|---|---|---|
| **A.** | To increase reading speed | _____ |
| **B.** | To increase comprehension of main ideas | _____ |
| **C.** | To improve vocabulary understanding | _____ |
| **D.** | To learn more about the information in this chapter | _____ |
| **E.** | To improve understanding of style and grammar | _____ |

# LOOKING AHEAD

In Chapter 1, you read about some of the changes that have taken place recently in various parts of the world. One result of these political changes is the movement of populations from one country to another. People seeking a new political or economic environment sometimes find different countries in which to live and work.

This chapter concerns the movement of the world's population and the role of immigration. Because the United States has long had the reputation for being a "nation of immigrants," many of the readings relate directly to the role of immigration in the U.S. The following titles are included in this chapter:

"Third World USA," by Ryzsard Kapuscinski

"New World," by Jonathan Raban

"Global Village"

"Lost Sister," by Cathy Song

*IT WORKS!*
*Learning Strategy:*
*Guessing*

1. What kinds of topics (specifically) would you guess will be covered in this chapter?
2. What do you know about immigration to the U.S.?
3. Do you think the world has an overpopulation problem?
4. Look ahead at the graphic material included in this chapter. What does it tell you about the subject matter?
5. What would you like to know about this topic? Write down two or three questions you have about the world's population.

## TRY A NEW STRATEGY

Keeping a journal of your thoughts, progress, and goals for learning English will help you to understand your own learning process. Make notes on your classwork as well as on what you learn outside of class.

## LISTENING

*IT WORKS!*
*Learning Strategy:*
*Listen to Learn*

With a group of classmates, find one of the following films in a local video store. *Moscow on the Hudson*, a film portraying the life of a Russian immigrant in New York, or *Dim Sum* the story of the cultural adjustment of a Chinese family in the U.S.

**1.** Use the following spaces to take notes as you watch the film.

The title of the film you watched:

_____

The names of the main characters:

_____

_____

_____

The important events in the story:

_____

_____

_____

_____

_____

_____

_____

_____

Describe your favorite scene:

_____

_____

_____

## Threads

**On an average day, 1,648 persons emigrate to the U.S., and 670 immigrants become naturalized American citizens.**

US Immigration &
Naturalization Service

*LEARNING STRATEGY*

**Understanding and Using Emotions: Discussing your feelings can help to clarify your thoughts about what you read or watch.**

2. Discuss the following questions with your partners.
   a. Did you like the movie you selected? Why or why not?
   b. What do you think the main idea of this film was? Explain your answers.
   c. How did this film make you feel? (For example, happy, sad, etc.) Why?
   d. On a scale of 1-10, with 10 being the best, what rating would you give this film? Why?

C. As a group, compile your answers and give a report to your class about the film you watched. Include in the report the details of the movie, how well your group liked it, and what your reactions to the film were.

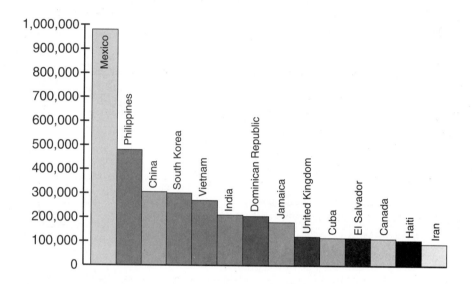

Documented Immigration to the U.S in the 1980s.[1]
Adapted from *The Universal Almanac 1991,* p. 204. Kansas City: Andrews and McMeel.

## ANALYSIS

With a partner, discuss the following questions concerning the graph above.

1. Look at the 14 countries that contributed most to immigration to the U.S. in the 1980s—are there any countries you are surprised to see on that list? Which ones?
2. What world events are you aware of that might have contributed to the immigration from some of these countries?

## PREREADING QUESTION

With a partner, discuss what you think the title "Third World USA" means.

---

[1]The number of Mexican immigrants increased dramatically in 1989 because a large number of undocumented immigrants (338,700) were given permanent resident status under the Immigration Reform and Control Act of 1986.

# THIRD WORLD USA

## Ryzsard Kapuscinski

America is becoming more diverse every day because of the unbelievable facility of new Third World immigrants to put a piece of their original culture inside American culture. The notion of a "dominant" American culture is changing every moment. It is incredible coming to America to find you are somewhere else—in Seoul, in Taipei, in Mexico City. You can travel inside Korean culture right on the streets of Los Angeles, for instance.

For an Eastern European, to come to America at the turn of the century was a very strong cultural shock. His connection to home was cut abruptly. Today, immigrants are living in one place physically, but they are sustained culturally from elsewhere. They can watch Mexican soap operas on TV, or regularly fly back and forth to Mexico on the cheap midnight flight out of Los Angeles International Airport. They can read Korean news at the same time it is being read in Seoul, and can take the daily jumbo jets to Korea. The freedom to have this sort of contact is culturally and psychologically healthy. Immigrants don't feel completely cut off from their past the day after their departure from home.

To live here, you don't even need to speak English. In Los Angeles there is an ever-growing sphere where you don't even hear the English language. You don't see it on the commercial signs, in advertising, in the local newspapers. You don't hear it on the radio or on the cable TV channels.

Recently I flew from Toronto to Philadelphia. It was late at night. My plane landed. Other planes were also just landing, from Miami, from Los Angeles. At this airport Cubans and Puerto Ricans were coming to meet the planes with their whole families. Lots of children were playing, slipping down, crying. My luggage was lost. Nobody could find anything. It was hot, crowded, noisy. A mess. There I was in Philadelphia, the historical American town, and I hadn't seen one white face. There was terrible disorder, the lost luggage, the cry of the children, Spanish language only, I said to myself, "I'm at home. I'm in the Third World."

Features of Third World society are penetrating American life. Third World influences—dynamic disorganization, easygoing attitudes, a slower pace of life, a different measurement of time and relations to family—are altering the once dominant northern European ways of putting society together. The sphere of neat, well-organized white society is shrinking.

The wrong angle to approach the new multicultural reality is from the perspective of Western cultural values, including Greek philosophy. Each culture has something to bring to the new pluralistic culture being created.

We can't say Western values are broken down. We are in a period of transition in which the notion of values is broader. We are departing from the time in which we accepted only one set of values as the truthful way of living. We are entering the period in which we will have to accept values that represent other cultures that are not "worse" than our values, but different. This transition is very difficult because our conditioning is ethnocentric. The mind of the future America, however, will be polycentric.

Source: *New Perspectives Quarterly*, Summer 1988.

## COMPREHENSION

Answer the following questions without looking at the reading. Fill in the blanks of each sentence with an appropriate word.

1. America is becoming diverse because of the ability of Third World immigrants to put a piece of their original _____ into American _____.

2. Eastern Europeans earlier in the century experienced _____ _____ because their ties with their homelands were cut off abruptly.

3. We are entering the period in which we will have to accept _____ that represent other _____ that are not "worse" than our _____, but different.

4. In Los Angeles there is an ever-growing sphere where you don't even hear _____.

---

### *LEARNING STRATEGY*

**Understanding and Using Emotions: Discussing your feelings can help you understand the learning process better.**

---

## ANALYSIS

1. **a.** List the reasons the author thinks that being an immigrant today is easier than it was before.

   _____

   _____

   **b.** List other reasons you think being an immigrant might be easier today than before.

   _____

   _____

   **c.** List reasons you think it might be more difficult for immigrants today than before.

   _____

   _____

*IT WORKS!*
*Learning Strategy:*
*Cultural Awareness*

2. Reread the final paragraph of this reading, then complete the following:
   **a.** Make a list of the advantages of accepting other cultures' value systems, in your opinion.

   _____

   _____

   **b.** Make a list of the disadvantages.

   _____

   _____

3. Describe how "foreign" cultures are regarded in your own country or culture.

_____

_____

4. Find a partner, preferably from a different culture from your own, and compare your lists. How are they different? The same?
5. Join another pair to form a group of four, and compare your answers again. Discuss your findings with the class.

## PREREADING ACTIVITY

*IT WORKS!*
*Learning Strategy:*
*Getting the Main Idea*

*IT WORKS!*
*Learning Strategy:*
*Visualization*

Quickly scan the following reading (that is, look at it quickly, for specific information) and look for words that you think might be important to the main idea of this story.

As you did in Chapter 1, try to visualize some of the scenes in this reading. When you see a star (☆) in the margins, pause and try to picture the description in your mind.

### NEW WORLD

*Jonathan Raban*

1    On that particular morning, in hotels and motels in furnished rooms and cousins' houses, 106 other people were waking to their first day as immigrants to Seattle. These were flush times, with jobs to be had for the asking, and the city was growing at the rate of nearly 40,000 new residents a year. The immigrants were piling in from every quarter. Many were out-of-state Americans: New Yorkers on the run from the furies of Manhattan; refugees from the Rustbelt[2]; Los Angelenos escaping from their infamous crime statistics, huge house-prices and jammed and smoggy freeways; and redundant farm workers from Kansas and Iowa. Then there were the Asians— Samoans, Laotians, Cambodians, Thais, Vietnamese, Chinese and Koreans, for whom Seattle was the nearest city in the continental United States. A local artist had proposed a monumental sculpture, to be put up at the entrance to Elliott Bay[3], representing Liberty holding aloft a bowl of rice.

2    The falling dollar, which had so badly hurt the farming towns of the Midwest, had come as a blessing to Seattle. It lowered the price abroad of the Boeing airplanes, wood pulp, paper, computer software and all the other things that Seattle manufactured. The port of Seattle was a day closer by sea to Tokyo and Hong Kong than was Los Angeles, its main rival for the shipping trade with Asia.

3    By the end of the 1980s, Seattle had taken on the dangerous luster of a promised city. The rumor had gone out that if you had failed in Detroit you might yet succeed in Seattle—and that if you'd succeeded in Seoul, you could succeed even better in Seattle. In New York and in Guntersville I'd heard the rumor. Seattle was the coming place.

4    So I joined the line of hopefuls.

5    Of all the new arrivals, it was the Koreans who had made the biggest, boldest splash. Wherever I went, I saw their patronyms on storefronts, and it seemed that half the small family businesses in Seattle were owned by Parks or

Kims. I picked up my trousers from the dry cleaner's at the back of the Josephinum, stopped for milk and eggs at a Korean corner grocery, looked through the steamy window of a Korean tailor's, passed the Korean wig shop on Pike Street, bought oranges, bananas and grapes from a Korean fruit stall in the market, and walked the hundred yards home via a Korean laundromat and a Korean news and candy kiosk.

☆

6    For lunch I went to Shilla, where I sat up at the bar, ordered a beer, and tried to make sense of the newspaper which had been left on the counter—the *Korea Times*, published daily in Seattle. The text was in Korean characters, but the pictures told one something. There were portrait photographs of beaming Korean-American businessmen dressed, like many of the restaurant's customers, in blazers, button-down shirts and striped club ties. Several columns were devoted to prize students, shown in their mortar boards°, and academic gowns. On page three there was a church choir. There was a surprising number of advertisements for pianos. I guessed that the tone of the text would be inspirational and uplifting: the Korean Times seemed to be exclusively devoted to the cult of business, social and academic success.

*a type of flat hat, worn by students at graduation ceremonies.*

☆

7    "You are reading our paper!" It was the proprietor of the restaurant, a wiry man with a tight rosebud smile.

☆

8    "No—just looking at the pictures."

9    He shook my hand, sat on the stool beside me and showed me the paper page by page. Here was the news from Korea; this was local news from Seattle and Tacoma; that was Pastor Kim's family-advice column; these were the advertisements for jobs. . .

10   "It is very important to us. Big circulation! Everybody read it!"

11   So, nearly a hundred years ago, immigrant Jews in New York had pored over the Jewish Daily Forward, the Yidishe Gazetn and the Arbeite Tseitung. They had kept their readers in touch with the news and culture of the old world at the same time as they taught the immigrants how to make good in the new. To the greenhorn° American, the newspaper came as a daily reassurance that he was not alone.

*an inexperienced person*

12   "You are interested?" the restaurateur said. "You must talk to Mr. Han. He is the president of our association. He is here—"

13   Mr. Han was eating by himself, hunched over a plate of seafood. In sweatshirt and windbreaker, he had the build of a bantamweight boxer. The proprietor introduced us. Mr. Han bowed from his seat, waved his chopsticks.

☆   Sure! No problem! Siddown!

14   His face looked bloated with fatigue. His eyes were almost completely hidden behind pouches of flesh, giving him the shuttered-in appearance of a sleepwalker. But his mouth was wide and awake, and there was a surviving ebullience° in his grin, which was unselfconsciously broad and toothy.

*enthusiasm* ☆

15   He gave me his card. Mr. Han was President of the Korean Association of Seattle, also owner of Japanese Auto Repair ("is big business!"). He had been in America, he said, for sixteen years. He'd made it. But his college-student clothes, his twitchy hands and the knotted muscles in his face told another story. If you passed Mr. Han on the street, you'd mistake him for a still shell-shocked newcomer; an F.O.B., as people said even now, long after the Boeing had displaced the immigrant ship. He looked fresh-off-the-boat.

16   The Chinese had been the first Asians to make a new life in Seattle. They called America "The Gold Mountain" and were eager to take on the hard, poorly paid jobs that were offered to them in the railroad construction gangs. For as long as it took to build the railroads, they were made welcome, in a mildly derisive way. Their entire race was renamed "John", and every John was credited with an extraordinary capacity to do the maximum amount of work on the minimum amount of rice. As soon as the railroads began to lay off workers, the

amiable John was reconceived as "a yellow rascal" and "the rat-eating Chinaman". During the 1870s, the federal legislature began to behave towards the Chinese much as the Tsars Alexander II and Nicholas II behaved towards the Jews in Russia. At the very moment when the United States was receiving the European huddled masses on its eastern seaboard, it was establishing something cruelly like its own Pale°, designed to exclude the Chinese from white American rights and occupations. The Geary Act prohibited the Chinese from the right to bail and habeas corpus.[4] In Seattle in 1886, gangs of vigilantes succeeded in forcibly deporting most of the city's Chinese population of 350 people; persuading them, with knives, clubs and guns, to board a ship bound for San Francisco.

*a boundary or fence, figuratively speaking here.*

☆

17    For the immigrant from Asia, the Gold Mountain was a treacherous rock face. No sooner had you established what seemed to be a secure foothold than it gave way under you. The treatment of the Seattle Chinese in 1886 was matched, almost exactly, by the treatment of the Seattle Japanese in 1942[5], when hundreds of families were arrested, loaded on trains and dispatched to remote internment camps.

18    Now, if you came from Asia, you could not trust America to be kind or fair. This particular week, if you went to an English class at the Central Community College, you would see spray-gunned on the south wall of the building SPEAK ENGLISH OR DIE, SQUINTY EYE! Peeing in a public toilet, you'd find yourself stuck, for the duration with a legend written just for you: KILL THE GOOKS

19    In the ghetto of Seattle's International District, a four-by-four block grid of morose, rust-colored tenements, there was at least safety in numbers. There was less pressure on the immigrant to get his tongue round the alien syllables of English. Even a professional man, like the dentist or optometrist, could conduct his business entirely in his original language. In the bar of the China Gate restaurant, I sat next to a man in his early seventies, born on Jackson Street, who had served with the United States Air Force in World War Two. He was affable°, keen to tell me about his travels and almost incomprehensible, Yi wong ding ying milding hyall!

☆

*friendly*

20    "You were in Mildenhall? In Suffolk?"

21    "Yea! Milding Hall!"

22    So, painfully, we swapped memories of the air base there. He didn't understand much of what I said, and I didn't understand much of what he said; yet his entire life, bar this spell in wartime England, had been passed in Seattle—or, rather, within the Chinese-speaking fifty-acre grid.

23    The Chinese, the Japanese, the Vietnamese, Laotians, and Cambodians had all established solid fortresses in, or on the edge of the International District. There were few Koreans here. There was the Korean Ginseng Center on King Street; there was a Korean restaurant at the back of the Bush Hotel on Jackson; some Koreans worked as bartenders in the Chinese restaurants.

24    In Los Angeles, there was a "Little Korea"; a defined area of the city where the immigrant could work for, and live with, his co-linguists, much as the Chinese did here in the International District. For Koreans in Seattle, though, immigration was, for nearly everyone, a solitary process. The drive to own their own businesses, to send their children to good schools, to have space, privacy, and self-sufficiency, had scattered them, in small family groups of twos and threes, through the white suburbs. They didn't have the daily solace of the sociable rooming house, the street and the café. For many, there was the once-a-week visit to church; for others there was no Korean community life at all.

It was this solitude that drew me to them. The Seattle Koreans knew, better than anyone else, what it was like to go it alone in America; and although I came from the wrong side of the world I could feel a pang of kinship for these people who had chosen to travel by themselves.

[2]A region of the U.S. where steel production was formerly the primary industry. Rustbelt refers to the current depression of that industry.
[3]A body of water in Seattle that is part of Puget Sound, a larger bay in the interior of the state of Washington.
[4]Habeas corpus` refers to the order by a judge to have a prisoner brought to court to determine the legality of the imprisonment.
[5]The U.S. government has recently paid $10,000 to Japanese who were imprisoned during World War II, by way of restitution for the property and jobs that they lost.

Source: Excerpted from *Granta 32*, Spring 1990, pg. 233–253.

## COMPREHENSION

Answer these questions without looking at the reading.

1. This reading concerns primarily the immigration of
   a. Laotians to Los Angeles;
   b. Koreans to Seattle;
   c. Chinese to San Francisco;
   d. Jews to New York.
2. Answer the following questions *true* or *false*.

   a. _____ The Koreans in Seattle settled in the International District with other Asian immigrants.

   b. _____ Seattle has a special section of town called "Little Korea."

   c. _____ Asians have migrated to Seattle because they were well-treated there.
3. Complete the following sentences.
   a. The Geary Act prohibited the Chinese from

   _____

   b. The _____ had been the first Asians to make a new life in Seattle.
      They called America _____.

## ANALYSIS

*Vocabulary*

In the following sentences, the italicized word is defined by another word or phrase somewhere else in the sentence. Circle the *synonym*.

1. Wherever I went, I saw their *patronyms* on storefronts, names like Park or Kim.
2. They didn't have the daily *solace* of the sociable rooming house, the comfort of a close community, or the advantages of other Asian immigrants.
3. In the International District there were many *morose*, rust-colored, depressing apartment buildings.

4. These were *flush* times, an era of prosperity, a period of happiness.
5. If you saw Mr. Han on the street, you'd mistake him for an *F.O.B.*; he looked fresh-off-the-boat.

*Working Together*

1. Reread paragraph 11, on page 30. How does this paragraph relate to the previous reading "Third World USA"?

## LEARNING STRATEGY

**Understanding and Using Emotions: Understanding others' thoughts, feelings, and experiences helps you better comprehend different ideas expressed in your readings.**

2. This reading and the one before it both deal with some of the difficulties of being an immigrant.

With a small group of classmates, discuss the difficulties described in these readings, as well as difficulties you personally know of involved in living in a new country. What kinds of service or help would have been useful to you as a newcomer to your community?

Next, imagine that your group forms a committee to help newcomers from other countries adapt to their new surroundings. Using the outline below, develop a plan for making life easier for new immigrants to your community.

The name of your organization _____

What services will you offer? _____

_____

_____

_____

How do you plan to contact new arrivals?

_____

_____

_____

What information will you publish? In what languages?

_____

_____

_____

Additional information

_____

_____

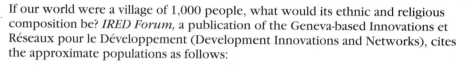

**Remembering New Material: Using physical action helps you to remember information.**

## PREREADING ACTIVITY

As you "read" the following numbers and data, try to create a graph or picture to help illustrate this information.

### THE GLOBAL VILLAGE

If our world were a village of 1,000 people, what would its ethnic and religious composition be? *IRED Forum,* a publication of the Geneva-based Innovations et Réseaux pour le Développement (Development Innovations and Networks), cites the approximate populations as follows:

In the village would be:
- 564 Asians
- 210 Europeans
- 86 Africans
- 80 South Americans
- 60 North Americans

There would be:
- 300 Christians (183 Catholics, 84 Protestants, 33 Orthodox)
- 175 Moslems
- 128 Hindus
- 55 Buddhists
- 47 Animists
- 1 Other
- 210 without any religion or atheist

Of these people:
- 60 would control half the total income
- 500 would be hungry
- 600 would live in shanty towns
- 700 would be illiterate

Source: Excerpted from World Development Form *(April 15, 1990)*

## PREREADING QUESTION

Before reading the next passage, answer the following questions. Work with a partner.

1. What does the word "refugee" mean?
2. Thinking about Chapter 1, how might changing political structures affect refugees? Can you think of any specific examples from recent news events?
3. What countries do you associate most with refugees?

**Managing Your Learning: Paying attention to specific details, rather than everything contained in a reading, can help increase your reading speed.**

This reading is taken from the *1991 Universal Almanac.* Scan it, that is read it quickly looking for specific information. Fill out the chart that follows it.

# World Refugees

International assistance to refugees was first organized in 1921, with the appointment of a League of Nations High Commissioner for Refugees. On Dec. 8, 1949, the UN General Assembly created the United Nations Relief Works Agency for Palestine Refugees in the Near East (UNRWA) to provide aid to Palestine refugees. International aid to other refugees is currently coordinated by the Office of the United Nations High Commissioner for Refugees (UNHCR), established in 1951 by the UN General Assembly. The UNHCR does not aid or count Palestine refugees. Many nongovernmental organizations also provide aid to refugees, · in cooperation with UNHCR and UNRWA and independently.

Exactly who is a refugee was defined in 1951 by the Convention Relating to the Status of Refugees as a person who "owing to well-founded fear of being persecuted for reasons of race, religion, nationality, membership of a particular social group, or political opinion is outside the country of his nationality and is unable or, owing to such fear, is unwilling to avail himself of the protection of that country; or who, not having a nationality and being outside the country of his former habitual residence as a result of such events, is unable or

owing to such fear, is unwilling to return to it." Because the 1951 convention covered only persons who became refugees up to Jan. 1, 1951, a Protocol Relating to the Status of Refugees was drafted and entered into force in 1967. The protocol extends the basic rights of the 1951 convention without the limitation of date. As of July 1, 1990, 103 countries were parties to the convention and 104 nations have acceded to the Protocol.

## CURRENT SITUATION

**UNHCR** During 1989 UNHCR provided aid to approximately 15 million refugees and was represented in more than 100 countries. Representatives from 43 countries (from all geographical regions) comprise the Executive Committee which supervises UNHCR's activities. UNHCR received the Nobel Peace Prize in 1954 and 1981.

**UNHCR** During 1989 UNRWA provided aid to approximately 2,334,000 registered Palestine refugees. Another 534,000 Palestine refugees are not registered with UNRWA. Members from 10 countries comprise the Advisory Commission which directs UNRWA's programs.

**New refugee restrictions** Increasingly throughout the 1980s the United States, Western Europe, Canada, and

Australia—the principal recipients of the world's refugees—have been rejecting asylum seekers by creating a wide range of new restrictive measures. Nations now fear an unending flow of people from impoverished lands who seek economic betterment, not political safety.

**Decreased funding** According to the *World Refugee Survey,* 1989 was characterized by less funding and less humanitarian leadership from the traditional donor countries—the United States, Western Europe, and others. The shortfalls are so severe that the condition of refugees has generally deteriorated, with nutritional and medical services curtailed and education and self-sufficiency programs essentially eliminated.

## REFUGEE CRISIS IN AFRICA

The Horn of Africa is currently the world's most troubled region in terms of the world-wide refugee crisis. Internal wars in Somalia and Sudan are uprooting millions and killing thousands. Major fighting in Tigray and Entrea in Ethiopia is now compounded by a major drought which may threaten five million people. Hundreds of thousands of people flee civil war in their own country only to be caught in war zones and famines in their asylum country.

**Ethiopia** According to official UNHCR figures, approximately 740,00 refugees—385,000 Sudanese and 355,000 Somalis—were registered in Ethiopia in 1989. Simultaneously, some 1,035,900 Ethiopians fled their war torn country to Somalia (350,000), Sudan (663,200) and in smaller numbers, Djibouti, Kenya, and Egypt.

**Sudan** A civil war has caused more than 425,000 Sudanese refugees to take refuge in neighboring Ethiopia and Uganda. During 1988 an estimated 300,000 southern Sudanese starved because both sides in the civil war used food as a weapon.

**Somalia** More than 385,000 Somali refugees have fled to neighboring countries. 355,000 to Ethiopia, and others to Djibouti and Kenya. Ethiopian refugees living in camps in northern Somalia continue to return to Ethiopia in numbers that are difficult to calculate. The U.S. Committee for Refugees estimates that 350,000 Ethiopian refugees were in Somalia in 1988.

**Mozambique** An estimated 1.7 million Mozambicans are internally displaced and another 2.9 million are partly or wholly dependent on food aid. 1.3 million Mozambicans have fled to neighboring countries during 1989. 15,000 fled each month to Malawi alone.

**Kenya** Kenya has recently changed its hospitable refugee policy. In April 1989 Kenyan authorities forcibly repatriated some 237 of its 600 Ugandan refugees. Somali refugees reportedly suffered beatings and were forced back across the border into Somalia where some were imprisoned or killed.

## COUNTRIES ACCEPTING MOST REFUGEES, 1975-88

The following table lists the 11 countries that officially accepted the most refugees for resettlement in 1975-88.

| Country | 1975-88 | 1968 |
|---|---|---|
| United States | 1,249,608 | 83,420 |
| Canada | 252,225 | 28,588 |
| France | 178,246 | 8,794 |
| Australia | 161,160 | 10,301 |
| Sweden | 84,354 | 17,601 |
| West Germany | 78,969 | 7,621[1] |
| Spain | 34,509 | 3,938 |
| Denmark | 28,733 | 2,196 |
| Switzerland | 20,666 | 680 |
| Austria | 18,501 | 1,785 |
| Netherlands | 17,416 | 2,301 |

## PRINCIPAL SOURCE COUNTRIES OF WORLD'S REFUGEES IN 1989

The following counts may understate the total number of refugees from a given country because asylum nations do not always specify the origin of their refugees.

| Country | Refugees |
|---|---|
| Afghanistan | 5,934,500[1] |
| Palestine | 2,340,500 |
| Mozambique | 1,354,000[1] |
| Ethiopia | 1,035,900[1] |
| Iraq | 508,000[1] |
| Angola | 438,000 |
| Sudan | 435,100 |
| Somalia | 388,600[1] |
| Cambodia | 334,166 |
| Iran | 270,100[1] |
| Rwanda | 233,000[1] |
| Burundi | 186,500[1] |
| Western Sahara | 165,000[1] |
| Vietnam | 124,779 |
| China (Tibet) | 112,000 |
| Sri Lanka | 103,000 |
| Nicaragua | 89,700[1] |
| Laos | 69,044 |
| Liberia | 68,000 |
| El Salvador | 61,100[1] |

*The Universal Almanac, 1991. J.W. Wright, General Editor. Kansas City: Andrews and McMeel.*

[1]Original sources vary significantly in numbers reported.

## WORLD REFUGEE SUMMARY

1. What are the full names of the following?

   UNRWA _____

   UNHCR _____

2. When did the following events take place?

   International assistance to refugees was first organized in _____

   UNRWA was established in _____

   UNHCR was established in _____

3. What is the official definition of "refugee"?

   _____

4. What are the main causes of refugees in these African nations?

   Ethiopia _____

   Sudan _____

   Somalia _____

   Mozambique _____

   Kenya _____

5. Which African country is the source of the most refugees?

   _____

6. What three countries accepted the most refugees?

   _____

7. What three countries were the source of the most refugees?

   _____

8. What were the new refugee restrictions imposed in several developed countries?

   _____

## PREREADING QUESTION

In your journal, or on another piece of paper, write a description of how you think your family feels about your, or another family member's, traveling to different parts of the world. Include in your description how you feel about being away from your home country.

*Read this poem to your-self, then read it aloud.*

## Lost Sister

### 1

In China, even the peasants
named their first daughters
jade—
the stone that in the far fields
could moisten the dry season,
could make men move mountains
for the healing green of the inner hills
glistening like slices of winter melon.

And the daughters were grateful:
They never left home.
To move freely was a luxury
stolen from them at birth.
Instead, they gathered patience,
learning to walk in shoes
the size of teacups,
without breaking—
the arc of their movements
as dormant as the rooted willow,
as redundant as the farmyard hens.
But they traveled far
in surviving,
learning to stretch the family rice,
to quiet the demons,
the noisy stomachs.

### 2

There is a sister
across the ocean,
who relinquished her name,
diluting jade green
with the blue of the Pacific.
Rising with a tide of locusts,
she swarmed with others
to inundate another shore.
In America,
there are many roads
and women can stride along with men.

But in another wilderness,
the possibilities,
the loneliness,
can strangulate like jungle vines.
The meager provisions and sentiments
of once belonging—
fermented roots, Mah-Jong tiles and firecrackers—set but
a flimsy household in a forest of nightless cities.
A giant snake rattles above,
spewing black clouds into your kitchen.
Dough-faced landlords
slip in and out of your keyholes,
making claims you don't understand,
tapping into your communication systems
of laundry lines and restaurant chains.

You find you need China:
your one fragile identification,
a jade link
handcuffed to your wrist.
You remember your mother
who walked for centuries,
footless—
and like her,
you have left no footprints,
but only because
there is an ocean in between,
the unremitting space of your rebellion.

*Cathy Song*

Source: New York: W.W. Norton Company.

## ANALYSIS

### LEARNING STRATEGY

**Forming Concepts: Breaking down larger phrases into smaller parts helps you understand difficult passages.**

Reread the poem again, and mark the following passages.
1. Underline any passage you didn't understand.
2. Place stars next to any lines that contain unfamiliar vocabulary items.
3. With a partner's help, break down these passages word by word, and discuss their possible meanings. Also, discuss the meanings of unfamiliar vocabulary items.

*IT WORKS!*
*Learning Strategy:*
*Use a Dictionary*

*LEARNING STRATEGY*

**Forming Concepts: By linking what you know in your first language with words in English, you gain better understanding.**

**4.** Choose one stanza of the poem and translate it into your first language. (This is hard! Do the best you can.) Which words or phrases were difficult to translate?

### VOCABULARY

This poem contains several compound words, or words made up of two separate words. Each word below belongs to a compound word found in this poem. Working with a partner, using the definitions given, put the compounds back together.

| cracker | hand | cup | key | fire | tea | land |
| cuffs | hole | farm | print | lord | foot | yard |

**1.** You can drink out of it: _____

**2.** You celebrate the New Year with it: _____

**3.** You find cows and horses there: _____

**4.** Collects your rent each month: _____

**5.** One way to open the door: _____

**6.** Used to restrain criminals: _____

**7.** You leave it in the sand: _____

## SUMMARY EXERCISES

## Themes

### DISCUSS

Write two questions you would like to ask your class concerning the theme of international immigration. In a class discussion, ask two different classmates your questions.

## DEBATE

*Melting Pot or Tapestry?*

The U.S. has often been called a "melting pot," a place where different cultures blend into one culture. Others see it as a tapestry, that is a place where many different cultures fit together, but each keeps its own characteristics.

Which do you prefer? Review the readings in this chapter to find support for your opinion. In a group of six, divide into two smaller groups each taking one side. Present arguments for your opinion. Each side should have the same amount of time to make its presentation.

## ROLE-PLAY

Look again at the description of Mr. Han in "New World." Think also of the sister that was described in the poem, "Lost Sister." With a partner, decide which role each of you would like to play. Then, create a dialogue between these two, one Korean man and one Chinese woman, who decided to come to the U.S. In your role-play, show why each decided to leave his or her homeland and travel to the U.S.

## WRITE

Think back to your first day in the U.S. or another foreign country. Make a list of all of the impressions you can remember. Using your list, write a short essay describing what you saw, how you felt, and what you did.

## The Cultural Dimension

1. Interview a recent immigrant to the U.S. Prepare at least five questions to ask about his or her experiences as a new member of U.S. society. Report the results of your interview to the class.
2. Interview a U.S. citizen about his or her feelings on immigration in the U.S. Prepare at least five questions that relate to the advantages or disadvantages of the current immigration policies and practices. Tape record your interview or take detailed notes. Compare your findings with those of a classmate. How were your results different? How were they the same?

### Threads

2.3 Million students with limited English are enrolled in US schools.

US Dept. of Education

## Self-Evaluation Questionnaire

Make a list of new ideas or words you learned from this chapter.

1. _____
2. _____
3. _____
4. _____
5. _____
6. _____
7. _____
8. _____
9. _____
10. _____

As you did in Chapter 1, think about the goals you set at the beginning of the chapter. How well did you perform? Review your progress, then rate yourself on how you did in each of the following areas. Give yourself the following ratings:

**5 excellent   4 good   3 average   2 fair   1 poor**

|  | RATING |
|---|---|
| **A.** Improved reading speed | _____ |
| **B.** Understood main ideas | _____ |
| **C.** Increased vocabulary understanding | _____ |
| **D.** Learned more about the topic of the chapter | _____ |
| **E.** Developed more understanding of style and grammar | _____ |

Compare your ratings with the objectives you set on the first page of this chapter.

# Food and World Hunger

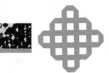

## PLANNING & GOALS

As in the two previous chapters, list in order of priority (with 1 as 'most important') the objectives that are important to you in this chapter.

| GOAL | RANK |
|------|------|
| **A.** To increase reading speed | _____ |
| **B.** To increase comprehension of main ideas | _____ |
| **C.** To improve vocabulary understanding | _____ |
| **D.** To learn more about the information in this chapter | _____ |
| **E.** To improve understanding of style and grammar | _____ |

## LOOKING AHEAD

We have seen in the first two chapters how political structures can affect groups of people. Food and its distribution, the subject of this chapter, is also an important factor in global organization. While many countries enjoy an abundance of food, other countries experience severe shortages of even basic staples, such as grain or vegetables. Achieving a balance is a problem continually addressed by the nations of the world.

Here are some of the readings you will find in this chapter, which address the questions of hunger, famine, world farming, and the marketing of food.

"Saving the Family Farm Can Benefit All of Us," by Frances Moore Lappé.

"Napa, California," a poem by Ana Castillo

"One Teen's Bout with Hunger," by Ellen Whitford

"Helping Africa End Its Famine," Interview with Hans Hurni

"Anatomy of a Cheeseburger," by Jeremy Rifkin

"Hamburger Diplomacy," by Boris Alexeyev

*IT WORKS!*
*Learning Strategy:*
*Cooperating*

Preview this chapter with a partner. Ask each other the following questions.

1. Which of the titles interest you most? Why?
2. What do you already know about the issue of hunger in the world?

3. What do you think can be done to solve the hunger problem in the world?
4. Have you ever eaten at a McDonald's restaurant outside of the U.S.? Inside the U.S.?
5. Write another question you would like to ask your partner here. Ask your partner your question. _____

_____

## Try a New Strategy

One way to become more confident about your reading skills is to recognize how much you already know about a topic. Before you begin this chapter, think about the subject of food distribution and world hunger, and make a list of everything you know about it. Include facts you know about your own country.

### LISTENING

As a class, contact a local relief agency, such as a soup kitchen or food bank. (Consult the yellow pages of the telephone book.) Ask a volunteer or other organizer to visit your class to talk about the work that the organization does in your community. Use the following information to help you write questions to ask your guest.

*IT WORKS!*
*Learning Strategy:*
*Listen to Learn*

1. The name of the agency
2. Its address and phone number
3. The type of help it provides
4. The type of people they help
5. The number of volunteers they need
6. Who may volunteer
7. Other questions

After the interview, write a letter thanking your guest for visiting.

Consider volunteering with a classmate to work for the agency you learned about. Report back to your class on your experience.

### *LEARNING STRATEGY*

**Managing Your Learning: Working with others is a good way to improve your language skills.**

### ANALYSIS

With a group of classmates, discuss the cartoon on the next page. Use the following questions, and any others you can think of.

## Calvin & Hobbes

Cartoon by Bill Watterson;
@ 1991 Andrews and
McMeel, A Universal Press
Syndicate Company.

*IT WORKS!*
*Learning Strategy:*
*Associating*

**a.** Did you find the cartoon is funny? Why or why not?

**b.** Why do you think the author made this cartoon?

## PREREADING QUESTION

Look at the title of this article. Before reading this passage, create a list of all the benefits of a family farm. (It might help to think of people you know who own family farms.)

_____

_____

_____

_____

_____

_____

_____

# SAVING THE FAMILY FARM CAN BENEFIT ALL OF US

## Frances Moore Lappé

Let's save the family farm—let's save it from what I call the nostalgia[1] argument. Farmers are special, the argument goes, because they cling to these old-fashioned notions of self-reliance. Can't we hold on to a little preserve of old-fashioned values while the rest of the economy yields to increasing concentration, which is considered so essential to "progress"?

No! Saving the family farm should have nothing to do with nostalgia, nor what is "special" about farmers. I am convinced that the issues raised by the demise of the family farm touch all Americans. The values at stake are widely shared throughout our society.

Farmers are thought of as a special breed because they desire freedom—flexibility and autonomy in their work; "being their own boss." In fact, most Americans want the same thing. In national opinion polls, the only people consistently reporting that they like their work are those who are self-employed. And about two-thirds of Americans say they would prefer to work for a worker-owned business.

What most Americans want in their own jobs is what has always been the basis of family farm agriculture: the opportunity for more self-direction, responsibility, and meaning in our work lives. Yet now, agriculture is moving in the opposite direction—for the first time in our history more than half of farm labor is performed by hired, not family, labor.

Similarly the *value* of community life is also presumed to be especially prized by rural people. The groundbreaking study on American values presented in the book *Habits of the Heart* (University of California, 1985) concludes that people's individualistic searches for satisfaction have left most Americans unfulfilled. What they seek, albeit inchoately[2], is a way to connect their own well-being to a sense of community purpose. Yet it is precisely these kinds of values that are being destroyed as small communities throughout America turn to ghost towns in the wake of accelerating concentration of farm ownership.

So let's get right to the heart of what is at stake. Are we mature enough as a society to put our values—democracy based on dispersed economic power, community based on a relative equality of condition—above the dogma of free market economics?

If so, rather than protecting farmers as relics of the past, we could view family farmers fighting for their livelihoods as heralds of the future—the vanguard of the movement working for greater democratization of economic life, which includes worker participation in management and worker ownership. We should promote farmers' demands to maintain their way of life as a critical first step toward fulfilling all Americans' wishes for meaningful work and renewed communities.

[1] Nostalgia means a feeling of desire for thing in the past. It often reflects a belief that the "old ways" were better.
[2] "Albeit inchoately" means "even if in a basic way."

Source: Excerpted from *Food First News*, Summer 1988, p. 2.

## COMPREHENSION

Without looking back at the reading. List all of the reasons the author gave for saving the family farm.

_____

_____

_____

_____

## ANALYSIS

1. With a partner, compare the lists you made before the reading with the ones you made in the "Comprehension" section above. What similarities and differences do you find?

2. The author quotes national opinion polls which say that "the only people [American] consistently reporting that they like their work are those who are self-employed." Why do you think this is? What advantages are there to being self-employed, rather than employed by someone else? What are the disadvantages? List them in the table below. Again, compare your answers to your partner's.

|  | SELF-EMPLOYMENT | EMPLOYMENT IN COMPANY |
|---|---|---|
| Advantages | _____ | _____ |
|  | _____ | _____ |
|  | _____ | _____ |
|  | _____ | _____ |
|  | _____ | _____ |
| Disadvantages |  |  |
|  | _____ | _____ |
|  | _____ | _____ |
|  | _____ | _____ |
|  | _____ | _____ |
|  | _____ | _____ |

## PREREADING ACTIVITY

The previous reading discussed the values of family farming. The following poem talks about a different experience—the migrant laborer working for large agricultural corporations. Before reading the poem, imagine what it would be like to spend your days in the fields. Write for five minutes on what this experience would be like. Don't worry about grammar or spelling! Just write whatever impressions come to your mind.

## Napa, California[1]

*Dedicado al Sr. Chávez, sept. '75*[2]

We pick
  the bittersweet grapes
  at harvest
  one
   by
    one
  with leather worn hands
      as they pick
      at our dignity
      and wipe our pride
      away
      like the sweat we wipe
      from our sun-beaten brows
      at midday
In fields
  so vast
  that our youth seems
  to pass before us
  and we have grown
  very
   very
    old
     by dusk. . .
     *(bueno pues, ¿qué vamos a hacer, Ambrosio?*
     *¡bueno pues, sequirle, compadre, sequirle!*
     *¡Ay, Mama!*
     *Si pues, ¿qué vamos a hacer, compadre?*
     *¡Seguirle, Ambrosio, sequirle!)*

We pick
  with a desire
  that only survival
  inspires
While the end
  of each day only brings
  a tired night
  that waits for the sun
  and the land
  that in turn waits
  for us. . .

                   *Ana Castillo*

A farm in Napa Valley, California.

*Well then, what are we going to do, Ambrosio?*
*Well then, follow him, friend, follow him!*
*Oh, Mama!*
*Yes, well, what are we going to do, friend?*
*Follow him, Ambrosio, follow him!*

*Ana Castillo was born in Chicago, Illinois, in 1953. She has been a magazine editor and a writer.*

Source: *Women are Not Roses,* Houston: Arte Publico Press: University of Houston Press, 1984.

[1] "The Grapes of Wrath" by John Steinbeck tells the story of a migrant farming family in the 1930s which travels from the Midwest to California. You can find this story either in book or video format.

[2] Translation: "Dedicated to Mr. Chávez, September 1975." "Mr. Chavez" refers to César Chávez, the founder of the United Farmworkers Union. He was born in San Jose, California in 1927 to a family of migrant farmworkers. During the 1960s and 1970s he led boycotts of grapes and lettuce, protesting the treatment of migrant farmworkers. He continues to be active in fighting for the rights of farmworkers.

## ANALYSIS

Discuss the following questions with a partner.

1. Why do you think the writer included words in Spanish in her poem?
2. What is the meaning of the word "bittersweet" (line 2). What does the author mean by "bittersweet grapes"?
3. There are three times of day mentioned: midday, dusk, and night. These times can also be interpreted as *metaphors*—things symbolizing something else. What might they be metaphors for? Why do you think morning is not mentioned in this poem?

## PREREADING ACTIVITY

Review the reading on refugees in the previous chapter. How are the topics of refugees and hunger related?

_____

_____

_____

_____

_____

_____

**Threads**

In 1990, the USA imported 5.8 trillion dollars worth of fruits and vegetables.

*US Department of Commerce*

*IT WORKS!
Learning Strategy:
Reviewing*

# ONE TEEN'S BOUT WITH HUNGER

*Ellen Whitford*

Most mornings when Angelo Chol wakes, he has no food to eat.

His first—and sometimes his only—meal of the day comes at noon. Each day, Angelo, 14, eats a bowl of porridge. Some days he also gets a bit of bread. Each day it is the same.

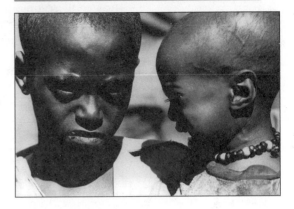

## Forced to flee

Four years ago, Angelo and his family were forced to flee from their home in southern Sudan. Armed tribesmen, fighting the Sudanese government in a civil war, had invaded Angel's village. They stole the villagers' cattle and burned most of the homes.

Angelo's father escaped, but no one knows where he is—or if he's still alive. With his mother, brothers, and sisters, Angelo came to northern Sudan, where there is no fighting. They live in a settlement outside of Khartoum, Sudan's capital. About 1.5 million people live in the makeshift refugee "towns" around Khartoum.

"When we arrived," Angelo says, "the first thing we did was build a small hut from sticks. To make walls and a roof, we covered the sticks with scraps of cardboard and plastic." Inside the hut, there is nothing but a burlap mat spread across the ground to sleep on. Because Angelo's family is so poor, they rarely have a morning meal. "Sometimes we have tea," says Angelo, "but most of the tea we have, my younger sister tries to sell to anyone who passes by our shelter."

Angelo gets his noon meal—his only certain meal of the day—at the school he attends. The porridge he eats is made of *dura*—a grain that has been boiled into a paste. "Sometimes, there is a little sugar to sweeten it, and a bit of flat bread," Angelo says. "If we are very lucky, we may also have some corn or tomatoes or onions. Vegetables are a treat."

At night, Angelo's family sometimes has a smaller meal of the same porridge. But unless his mother is lucky and finds work cleaning houses or washing clothes, they do not have money enough for food.

## Others starve

Yet Angelo considers his family fortunate. Every day, more people join the others in the settlements. They, too, have fled the civil war. The newcomers tell grim tales of others who were too weak to flee. Wandering, searching desperately for food, they starve to death.

Angelo is not starving here. International relief agencies supply some food for those in the settlements who have nothing to eat. But for years, day after day, Angelo has gone hungry.

He has grown accustomed to being hungry. The gnawing stomach pains last a few days. Eventually, they disappear, replaced by headaches. Angelo is always tired. And, with too little to eat, his body cannot fight off diseases. As a result, malaria, diarrhea, and intestinal parasites are common where he lives.

At first, Angelo thought about food all the time. Now, he does not like to think—or talk about—food at all. Angelo says he does not know if the war in his country will ever end. And he does not know if his family will ever have land again to grow crops. He says there is nothing he can do to change things. So, he must simply accept his hunger. For Angelo Chol, hunger is a way of life.

Source: *Scholastic Update*, Jan. 27, 1989, p. 3.

## COMPREHENSION

Answer these questions without looking back at the reading. Fill in the blanks of the passage with appropriate words (one word per blank).

At first, Angelo _____ about _____ all the time. Now, he does not like to think—or talk about—_____ at all. Angelo says he does not know if the _____ in his country will ever end. And he does not know if his _____ will ever have _____ again to grow _____ He says there is _____ he can do to change things. So, he must simply accept his _____. For Angelo Chol, hunger is a way of _____.

## ANALYSIS

Imagine that you are Angelo Chol. What would your day be like? Write a story describing a typical day in the life of Angelo Chol. Exchange stories with a classmate and reach each other's writing. Discuss your stories, and how your typical day is different from Angelo's.

## LEARNING STRATEGY

**Forming Concepts: Creating a map or drawing of related ideas enables you to understand the relationships between words.**

## PREREADING ACTIVITY

Think about the word *hunger*. What other words or phrases do you associate with *hunger*? Use the space below to show the relationship of those words to *hunger*, by drawing in boxes, arrows, circles, anything you like. The word "famine" has already been added for you.

hunger ⟶ famine

# HELPING AFRICA END ITS FAMINE

*Sylvia Honer*

This is an interview with Hans Hurni, who has been involved for 10 years with the Directorate for Cooperative Development and Humanitarian Help, part of the Swiss Ministry of Foreign Affairs, which is conducting research in Ethiopia, Kenya and Madagascar. The interview is conducted by Silvia Honer, from the *Tages-Anzeiger°* of Zurich, Switzerland. (The questions are labeled "Q", and the answers "A".)

*a Swiss newspaper*

**Q: Every two years we hear calls for help from Africa. Why are there always new famines?**

A: I would like to mention two causes. The first is the way that Africa has developed backward over the past 20 years. Per-capita food production has diminished, and economic growth has not been able to keep pace with the rise in population. Then there are such environmental problems as soil erosion, water contamination, and desertification°. These problems contribute to the fact that the production of food supplies cannot meet even the minimum requirements of the population. The second cause is the civil wars that have been raging in quite a few countries for 10, 20, or even 30 years.

*the changing of fertile land into desert*

It is, however, worth distinguishing between hunger and famine. Countless people suffer from hunger or chronic undernourishment in nearly all the large cities of the Third World. Famine, on the other hand—where people die in the thousands if no help comes from outside—exists nowadays really only in Africa, and there only in the rural areas. The peasants who live in such areas provide for themselves and are therefore not tied into a system of economic exchange that would compensate for deficits or crop failures.

**Q: The countries that now are in most urgent need of food assistance are experiencing civil war. Does assistance help keep not only the people but also the wars alive?**

A: This conjecture cannot be excluded. Food assistance that allows people to just barely survive but does not allow the standard of living to be raised also maintains the dissatisfaction.

**Q: Assistance can also prevent the level of dissatisfaction from becoming great enough to lead to massive protests. In this regard it may well support the ruling regimes.**

A: Indeed. The majority of African regimes are totalitarian. Food assistance can help these regimes provide the minimum necessary for survival so that unmanageably large problems do not develop. When I asked Ethiopian peasants where aid supplies came from, they never said that they came from World Vision or Oxfam. Rather, they said, "President Mengistu Haile Mariam [who was ousted in May]"—that is, the government. Relief supplies are often perceived not as international assistance but as assistance from the government. This, of course, can promote goodwill among the peasants toward the government that, in fact, oppresses them.

---

**Threads**

**Five Largest Food Crops in the World (in millions of tons):**
**Wheat, 445**
**Rice, 400**
**Corn, 392**
**Potatoes, 226**
**Barley, 162**

United Nations Environmental Program

**Q: How should one respond to this problem? No more food assistance, in the hope that such governments will be toppled sooner and the wars will then perhaps end?**

A: This is a dilemma. But you cannot simply give up. It is the industrialized nations' moral obligation to help people who are hungry. The Earth still produces enough for everyone.

At the same time, there should be intervention in the case of these governments. The United Nations has not used its power in the arbitration of conflicts between the ethnic groups or civil-war opponents in Africa. Instead, it has fallen back on the principle of non-interference in internal conflicts. The UN will have to play a more active role in the future. It must intervene in national conflicts and push for peace.

**Q: What kind of international assistance would encourage real development?**

A: One idea is to establish partnerships: A rich industrial nation commits itself to an active, long-term cooperative effort with a poor country in the South. The rich country could, for instance, support the treasury of the partner nation on a long-term basis and at the same time play a mediating role in the resolution of this nation's conflicts. All of this would have to occur in conjunction with the UN and without any profit to the rich country, lest a colonial relationship develop. In addition, raw materials and agricultural products from the Third World will have to fetch better prices.

**Q: Would certain conditions have to be met by the African nations in exchange for assistance? There is, after all, a great sense of disillusionment concerning the corruption and incompetence of African governments.**

A: Demands, yes, but one must give due consideration to what a country on the very bottom can truly accomplish. Democracy presupposes a consciousness in each and every individual that can view the interests of the collective state. This requires education and access to information. A peasant living in isolation hardly possesses this consciousness.

If the International Monetary Fund and the World Bank demand an open market and free trade from such countries, it would be a fatal blow to these governments. In Madagascar, where the World Bank imposed conditions, the state can hardly pay the salaries of its own employees any longer. "Open market" means that Madagascar has to compete on the world market. Its mountainous terrain, however, will not allow for large-scale cultivation. The growing of coffee in remote mountain valleys, where it takes days just to bring the harvest to the nearest roadway, is not profitable.

Ecological and societal conditions must be taken into account before an attempt is made to impose demands. Far too little is known of what goes on in these "mysterious" rural areas and of what it means to live as a subsistence farmer who is dependent on the weather and the soil.

**Q:** **As one of the major causes of the ever-recurrent famines you mention the subsistence economy, which is still widespread in Africa. There is no commercial service sector and hardly any impetus toward industrialization. How is it that no such development has taken place in Africa?**

**A:** In the drive toward global development, Africa missed the boat. Europe was able to become strong only because it had markets first in its own border regions and later on other continents. Japan, China, Thailand, and South Korea, for instance, produce goods that can be marketed in Europe and in the Third World. There is no place else for Africans to market primitive industrial goods. Thus, Africa no longer has the opportunity of working its way up through its own efforts. That is why Africa needs fairer treatment from us. Increased funding is needed as well as know-how and international pressure on governments.

**Q:** **If Africa were to become an international hardship case, would it still be able to adopt its own independent course of development and its own internal African market?**

**A:** If the international community is prepared to offer the sub-Saharan African countries massive economic, structural, and political support for 20 years or longer, there will be a chance for independence. The development of an internal African market depends on how aggressively we are determined to look after our own economic interests, or whether we will allow for other, less competitive produces. Solely from the perspective of global ecology, the only economic order that has a chance is one that limits the exchange of goods to the shortest possible distances. The formation of economically self-sufficient regions is thus not merely in Africa's interest—it is also central to our own long-term survival. If the African nations succeed at getting a handle on their population explosion, the destruction of the environment, the political immaturity of their citizens, and their economic dependence on us, the continent will have as good a future as we do.

*World Press Review,* July 1991, pp. 14-15.

**Overcoming Limitations: Asking questions is a good way to overcome limitations and get the information you need.**

*IT WORKS!*
*Learning Strategy:*
*Remembering*

## COMPREHENSION

Working with a partner, adopt the roles of interviewer and Mr. Hurni, activist for international assistance. The interviewer should read the questions given in the interview, and the person taking Mr. Hurni's role should try to answer those questions *without looking at the text.* (The exact words are not important; try to remember the message of his answers). When halfway through the questions, switch roles. The answerer may ask for help, and the questioner may give small clues to the answer.

*IT WORKS!*
*Learning Strategy:*
*Associating*

## PREREADING ACTIVITY

With a partner, write a detailed description of a McDonald's hamburger. (If you have never eaten a McDonald's hamburger, find a partner who has.) Be very specific: what size, color, taste, ingredients, etc. Read your description to the class. As you listen to others' descriptions, make notes of any details you may have overlooked.

## ANATOMY OF A CHEESEBURGER

*Jeremy Rifkin*

*1863-1947, American automobile manufacturer*

Ray Kroc, one of the founders of the McDonald's hamburger chain, changed American eating habits as effectively as Henry Ford° changed the way Americans travel. He understood the vast market created by highways and suburbs; the new form of transportation required a new kind of food—fast—and by the mid-1950s the hamburger had clearly become the premier fast food in the United States, eclipsing the previous national `dish`, the American apple pie. Today, 200 Americans purchase one (or more) hamburgers every second, and each American consumes twenty-seven-and-a-half pounds of ground beef every year.

*a catechism normally refers to a religious "instruction book"; in this case, the instruction book is secular, that is, non-religious*

Ray Kroc first sited his restaurants near churches, wanting to create a hamburger sanctuary: a place where pilgrims could rest and be refreshed, knowing that everything would be orderly and predictable, according to secular catechism°. Uniformity and speed were the important features: the process of making a hamburger was broken into components, and each task was written out in precise detail. Nothing was to be left to personal initiative or guesswork. There was a 385-page operating manual, McDonald's bible, and deviation from it was never tolerated.

Kroc began by standardizing beef patties: each one was to weigh 1.6 ounces, measuring 3.875 inches in diameter and contain no organs or grains. The bun was to be three and a half inches wide, high in sugar content so that it would brown quickly. There wold be a quarter of an ounce of onion.

Kroc left nothing to chance. In his memoir he recalls the care paid to the choice of wax paper used to separate the hamburger patties:

> It had to have enough wax on it so that the patty would pop off without sticking when you slapped it on to the griddle. But it couldn't be too stiff or the patties would slide and refuse to stack up. There was also a science in stacking the patties. If you made the stack too high, the one on the bottom would be misshapen and dried out. So we arrived at the optimum stack, and that determined the height of our meat supplier's packages.

Henry Ford said of his Model T, "I don't care what color they want as long as it's black." The same principle of uniformity could have applied to Kroc's hamburgers. Each one was the same, *always,* and customers were discouraged from garnishing theirs according to individual taste: to do so would slow up the line, and increase the expense of production. In his memoirs Kroc is adamant:

> The minute you get into customizing, you're on an individual basis. The cost of the product is exactly the same, but the labor triples. We can't do that.

Kroc allocated "fifty seconds" to serve a McDonald's hamburger, shake and fries.

Source: *Granta* 38 Winter 1991, pp. 88-89.

## COMPREHENSION

Answer these questions without looking back at the reading passage.

1. According to the reading, how are Ray Kroc, the founder of MacDonald's, and Henry Ford, the automobile manufacturer, alike?
   a. their belief in uniformity in production
   b. their insistence on quick production
   c. their popularity with the American public
   d. their development of production manuals
2. Why did Mr. Kroc want to discourage customers from garnishing their hamburgers according to individual taste?
   a. He patterned himself after Henry Ford.
   b. Too many ingredients needed to be ordered specially.
   c. It increased the cost of labor.
   d. They would become too demanding.
3. What was the American "national dish" before the hamburger?
   a. hot dogs
   b. french fries
   c. apple pie
   d. ice cream

## ANALYSIS

1. The reading indicates that the average American eats 27.5 pounds of ground beef per year, or approximately 1.25 ounces of ground beef per day—nearly the size of one McDonald's hamburger. Ask a classmate:

    **a.** How much beef do you think is eaten per day in your country?

    **b.** Are there many vegetarians in your country?

2. Although the reading indicates that Americans eat a large amount of beef, American eating habits are changing, and less beef is consumed now. With a partner, interview a resident of the U.S. about his or her eating habits. Think of at least 10 questions you would like to ask. Write those questions here.

    **a.** _____

    **b.** _____

    **c.** _____

    **d.** _____

    **e.** _____

    **f.** _____

    **g.** _____

    **h.** _____

    **i.** _____

    **j.** _____

    Write down the answers to the questions, then compare your answers with those of your classmates. What differences did you notice? What similarities?

## PREREADING ACTIVITY

Keep the previous reading in mind as you read this article about MacDonald's in Moscow.

*One way to improve your reading is to work in your ideal environment. Where do you read best? In quiet, or with music? In the morning or afternoon? Try to set up the ideal conditions for reading.*

# HAMBURGER DIPLOMACY

## Boris Alexeyev

"If you sit on your hands and wait for someone to come up with proposals, you risk wasting the rest of your life. Apart from your ideas, you need persistence, patience, and more patience. Only then will you be a success. Since we started negotiations in this country, several leaders have come and gone in the Soviet Union," the man sitting opposite me says as he sips strong tea from a paper cup. The man knows what he's talking about. He's George Cohon, the successful businessman who is one of the top men at McDonald's. Over his 14-year-long effort to strike a deal with the USSR to open a McDonald's restaurant in Moscow, Cohon has spent thousands of hours talking to hundreds of officials in various Soviet ministries.

In spite of bureaucratic putoffs and lack of coordination, Cohon never gave in to despair. In January 1987 his efforts received a powerful impetus. Cohon associates that with Mikhail Gorbachev, who threw his support behind a new Soviet law allowing the establishment of joint ventures with foreign capital. By April 1988 Cohon's team had signed a contract on opening a McDonald's in Moscow.

The Soviet partner in the project is Mosobshchepit Trust, which currently manages 9,200 restaurants, cafés, and cafeterias in schools, colleges, universities, factories, and plants.

"Every day," says Vladimir Malyshkov, general director of Mosobshchepit and co-chairman of the board of the joint venture Moscow-McDonald's, "the trust serves over eight million hot meals and 50 million cups of tea and coffee. Even so, it doesn't meet the demand."

Malyshkov is confident that the new project will be a success. He hopes that restaurants from overseas not only will shorten the lines at other Soviet eateries, but also will introduce new cuisines to the Soviet public and will provide first-rate training for Mosobshchepit, which over the years the Muscovites have given the dubious honor of being the "provider of hide-and-seek services."

Malyshkov willingly gave me all the facts about the new joint venture, except the financial aspects.

It's always a mystery to me why Soviet business people are reluctant to discuss the monetary aspects of their projects. Malyshkov was no exception in this regard.

"Let's just say that we've invested a lot of money," he said vaguely. His partner George Cohon, the co-chairman representing McDonald's, was far more open.

Cohon told me that investments in the project had amounted to 50 million dollars—40 million to set up a food production and distribution center, another 4.5 million to modernize the premises, and the remainder to train personnel.

Fifty-one per cent of the capital belongs to the Soviet side; the remainder 49 per cent to the foreign partner.

The lion's share of the hard currency investment has gone into setting up the food production and distribution center, which was built in the town of Solntsevo in the suburbs of Moscow.

Lyudmila Sviridova, 25, is a chemical engineer. She supervises the quality of the french fries produced by one of the production lines of the Solntsevo Food Center.

By the way, the Russet Burbank potato variety used for the fries has never been cultivated in the USSR before. Since the spring of 1989 this variety has been sowed on four collective farms in Moscow Region. The new technology employed to harvest the potatoes has put the yield at twice the average for Moscow Region. This year as many as 250 hectares will be sowed with the American potato.

Every half hour Lyudmila checks the quality of the french fries and approves their delivery to the counter. It's a monotonous job, but the pay is good. Lyudmila makes 400 rubles a month and hopes to make a career with McDonald's. She is scheduled to receive a pay raise after a specific period of time. Her earnings are not bad, considering the national average per worker is 240 rubles a month.

All products processed by the Solntsevo Food Center come from collective and state farms in Moscow Region. Every hour Solntsevo processes 50 kilograms of meat and 3,000 liters of milk and makes 5,000 apple pies. The ingredients obtained locally are up to McDonald's standards.

The new McDonald's restaurant is located in the very center of the Soviet capital, in Pushkin Square, where the former Lira Café used to be. Once a popular eating place of Muscovites, the Lira lost much of its appeal over the years, eventually taking on the look of an unattractive snack bar.

McDonald's was serious about modernizing the premises. The new restaurant can accommodate 700 eat-in customers. Another 200 will be able to eat outdoors on the patio in the summer. This new McDonald's sets a record for the company in size; it's the largest Golden Arches in the world.

The restaurant is capable of serving 15,000 customers a day. The opening day crush, however, exceeded all expectations. On the first day of business the staff served 30,000 eager customers, breaking another company record.

The 600 members of McDonald's Moscow staff were selected from 27,000 applicants. One of the lucky ones was Yelena Polyachek, a fourth year student at the Moscow Teachers Institute. Yelena recalls that the hiring committee was very selective. Interviews were followed by a four-week training course geared to help the staff cope with the busy pace of work.

The main attraction of the job is the hours, from a minimum of three to an undefined maximum. Schedules are flexible, and workers get free meals. Yelena receives 1.5 rubles an hour. By the end of the month that adds up to what is a sufficient sum from a student's point of view. Many of her fellow workers are university students; others are homemakers.

Unlike other joint ventures that deal solely in hard currency, the Moscow McDonald's displays a large sign on its doors: "Rubles Only."

I asked Cohon how he planned to spend his rubles.

"We're hoping that the restaurant will have catered to from five to six million customers before the year is out. The rubles will come in handy," Cohon answered, "since we're planning to open another 19 restaurants in Moscow. For that, we'll need a sufficient ruble capital. So we're

not concerned about how to deal with the lines outside our doors."

Here's what customers pay:

* Big Mac, soft drink, ice cream—5 rubles 65 kopecks; and
* Double hamburger, soft drink, ice cream—4 rubles 65 kopecks.

The meals aren't cheap for the ordinary Muscovite, but the cost hasn't scared off the people in line. The official exchange rate—one that does not reflect the real situation—is approximately one dollar for 60 kopecks.

The opening of the Moscow McDonald's was noted in *Izvestia* by Stanislva Kondrashov, a frequent contributor to *Soviet Life* magazine. In my view, his article reflects the apprehensions that are often voiced in Soviet media. In particular, Kondrashov writes:

Having sold dozens of billions of Big Macs and having become a habit for hundreds of millions of people, McDonald's is yet another triumph of the American business approach.

It is quite a contrast to our sweeping ideas that have never gotten off the ground, such as introducing the world market to our Russian kvass or Siberian *pelmeni* (meat dumplings).

McDonald's has arrived in the USSR in the first place because it has been able to keep its preset standard of quality, hygiene, and organization.

I don't know whether or not the management of the joint venture is aware of the tests that await it in Moscow. One of the main ones is that the project may be swept away by crowds of customers and inquisitive people. Another test, which is even more serious, is to maintain its standards and not reduce its quality. Will McDonald's be able to guard itself against the pitfalls that have swallowed up other ventures?

Only time will tell. . . .

Source: *Soviet Life*, June 1990, pp. 21-22.

## COMPREHENSION

Answer these questions without looking back at the reading.

1. What is the Mosobshchepit Trust?
   a. the building where the McDonald's is found in Moscow
   b. the Russian partner in the Moscow McDonald's venture
   c. the business that supplies the Moscow McDonald's employees
   d. the supplier of beef and potatoes to the Moscow McDonalds

2. What is the main attraction of a job at McDonald's in Moscow?
   a. the hours
   b. the free meals
   c. the salary
   d. the modern facilities

3. Which of the following statements does NOT describe the Moscow McDonald's?
   a. It's the biggest in the world.
   b. It had the largest crowd ever on opening day.
   c. Hard currency, such as the U.S. dollar, is not accepted.
   d. It imports American beef and potatoes.

4. Why does Mr. Malyshkov think the Moscow MacDonald's will be successful?
   a. It will shorten the lines at Moscow restaurants, and will introduce new cuisines to the public.
   b. It charges reasonable prices for good meals, and accepts all forms of currency.
   c. It is funded primarily by Americans, and employs experienced restaurant workers.
   d. It has a good location, and imports quality foods from the U.S..

## ANALYSIS

With two other students, gather the following information. (Each person in the group might be required to get a different piece of information.)

*IT WORKS!*
*Learning Strategy:*
*Cooperating*

1. a. Look in a current newspaper for the exchange rate for the Russian ruble: rubles per dollar (there are 100 kopecks in a ruble).
   b. What are the U.S. prices of the following McDonald's menu items (go to a local McDonald's to find out.)

| **American Price** | **Russian Price** (from reading) |
|---|---|
| _____ Big Mac | _____ Big Mac |
| _____ medium soft drink | _____ medium soft drink |
| _____ ice cream sundae | _____ ice cream sundae |

2. What is the current salary at MacDonald's? (Call or ask the manager.) How does that compare to the rate the Russian worker gets?

3. Together, write a short report on your findings, and present it to your class.

## Themes

### DISCUSSION

Write one question you would like to ask your class concerning the themes presented in this chapter.

_____

_____

_____

In a class discussion, ask a classmate your question. Make notes of the questions and answers presented in your class discussion.

### DEBATE

From the class discussion, in a group of four or more students, develop a topic for debate. Divide your group into two equal parts. Half of your group should argue for one side of the issue you chose, and the other side should argue for the other. Use the following table to help you develop your arguments.

Topic

_____

_____

State your side's opinion in one sentence.

_____

_____

_____

What are the reasons you believe this? (Again, state each reason as a sentence.)

1. _____

_____

2. _____

_____

3. _____

_____

## Threads

**Foods which originated in North & South America: Corn, Potato, Tomato, Chocolate, Vanilla, Peanut, Pineapple, Chili Pepper, Cassava Root**

4. _____

_____

(Use an additional piece of paper if you need more space.)

Present your debate to the class. Each side should get the same amount of time to present its arguments.

## ROLE-PLAY

A persona is different from a traditional role-play. In creating a persona, you choose the person you would like to play: his or her age, occupation, appearance, and so forth. On your own, develop a persona. Make notes of all the characteristics of that person. Part of your persona should include some element having to do with food or its production: you could take on persona of a farmer, or a relief worker, or a McDonald's manager. Anyone you would like to be. In your written description, be very precise, so that you get a good picture of what that person is like.

In class, with a group of three or more students, imagine you have read three different stories in the newspaper. React to each of those stories as your personal would.

**Story 1**: Your government has decided that it will enact a campaign to decrease the amount of beef that its citizens eat.

**Story 2:** Three new fast food restaurants will open in your city.

**Story 3:** Your government has decided to give many millions of dollars in aid to help famine-stricken countries.

## WRITING

Food is important not only to sustain life, but for cultural and social reasons as well. Write a short essay explaining the role food plays in your own culture. Include details of any particular celebrations or festivals that include food (for example, in the U.S. it is traditional to serve cake in honor of someone's birthday). Exchange essays with someone from another culture and read each other's reports. Discuss the similarities and differences you found.

When the delicate balance of rain and sun is upset, a drought can dry out the land and blow away the top soil.

*IT WORKS!*
*Learning Strategy:*
*Develop Cultural*
*Awareness*

## The Cultural Dimension

**1.** Interview a classmate about the hunger problems that might exist in his or her home country. (If there aren't any problems in this area, ask how the government has achieved this.) Prepare at least five questions to ask about this topic. Report on your interview to the class.

**2.** Interview U.S. citizens about the problems of hunger in the U.S.. Prepare at least five questions about this topic. Tape record your interview or take detailed notes. Write a report on the results of your interview.

## Self-Evaluation Questionnaire

Make a list of new words or ideas you learned from this chapter.

_____

_____

_____

_____

_____

_____

_____

_____

_____

_____

_____

_____

As you did in previous chapters, think about the goals you set at the beginning of the chapter. How well did you perform? Review your progress, then rate yourself on how you think you did in each of the following areas for this chapter. Give yourself the following ratings:

**5 excellent   4 good   3 average   2 fair   1 poor**

| | RATING |
|---|---|
| **A.** Improved reading speed | _____ |
| **B.** Understood main ideas | _____ |
| **C.** Increased vocabulary understanding | _____ |
| **D.** Learned more about the topic of the chapter | _____ |
| **E.** Developed more understanding of style and grammar | _____ |

Compare your ratings with the objectives you set on the first page of this chapter.

# *War*

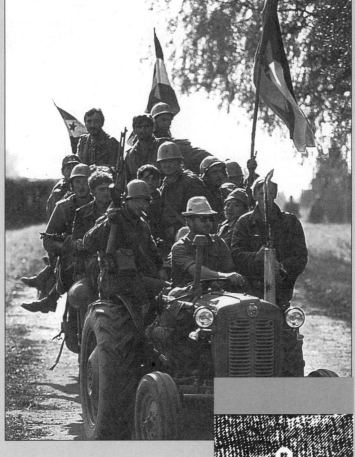

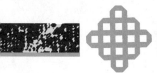

## PLANNING & GOALS

As in the previous chapters, list in order of priority (with 1 as 'most important') the objectives that are important to you in this chapter.

| GOAL | RANK |
|------|------|
| **A.** To increase reading speed | _____ |
| **B.** To increase comprehension of main ideas | _____ |
| **C.** To improve vocabulary understanding | _____ |
| **D.** To learn more about the information in this chapter | _____ |
| **E.** To improve understanding of style and grammar | _____ |

## LOOKING AHEAD

Few people desire war, but many people live with it daily. Wars arise for many different reasons, but frequently result in the same consequences: changing political boundaries, emigration, and famine. Yet, every day, somewhere in the world, there is a war.

The following readings address the issue of war in diverse areas of the world.

"Eye for an Eye" (Northern Ireland), by N. Richardson & G. Peress

"Beirut Diary" (Lebanon), by R. Fisk

"Grass" a poem by Carl Sandburg

"I was Far From Confident" (World War II), by Z. Abe

"The Man from Hiroshima" (World War II), by M. Chierici

"*Newsweek* War Edition" (advertisement) (Gulf War)

"Gregory" (Cyprus), by P. Ioannides

*IT WORKS!*
*Learning Strategy:*
*Guessing*

1. Do you think we are currently living in wartime or peacetime? Why do you feel this way?
2. Which of the titles above interest you the most?
3. Look ahead at the graphic material included in this chapter. What does it tell you about the subject matter?

## Try a New Strategy

Music plays an important role in language and culture. Many songs have been written about the subject of war. Locate a war song and listen to it, trying to understand the words. Think about how its theme relates to the readings in this chapter. Write a paragraph or two about your impressions of the song you found.

### LISTENING

Hundreds of movies have been made about wars. Research in a local video store or use a video guide (you can find one in the library) and find three titles that have treated each of the following wars:

**i.** Vietnam _____

_____

_____

**ii.** World War II _____

_____

_____

**iii.** World War I _____

_____

_____

**iv.** US Civil War _____

_____

_____

**v.** The French Revolution _____

_____

_____

With a partner or small group, check out and watch one or more of these films, and report on it to your class. Use the following questions to guide your report.

**1.** The name of the movie you watched:

_____

2. What were the names of the main actors in the film, and what were the names of the characters they played?

ACTOR                                    CHARACTER

_____        _____

_____        _____

_____        _____

_____        _____

3. Which war was treated in the film?

_____

4. Describe the story of the film, briefly. _____

_____

_____

5. Describe a memorable scene from the film. Try to recall all the details you can.

_____

_____

_____

6. Did you like the movie? Why or why not?

_____

_____

_____

7. Would you recommend that others see this film? _____

8. On a scale of one to ten (with ten being best), what rating would you give this film? _____

## Threads

**54.8 million people were killed in World War II (1939-1945).**

## PREREADING ACTIVITY

This reading takes place in Northern Ireland, but shares many details with the reading after it which takes place in Beirut. As you read, think about the similarities between the two stories. Also, try to visualize the scenes described here. Once again, pause at the stars (☆) in the margin and try to imagine what the scene looks like.

### EYE FOR AN EYE

*Nan Richardson and Gilles Peress*

☆ Belfast. There was a sound of glass breaking all over the city and a roar. Nine bomb blasts went off simultaneously in Belfast and five other cities: Newry on the border; Armagh; Londonderry; Portadown, the industrial city; and Lisburn, the Protestant northern enclave.

We drive slowly around the square. The damage is awesome—one million pounds of rubble, created in an instant with all nine bombs timed within seconds, synchronized to explode when no one was around. No one hurt, no one killed. Just a warning. The preliminary to a massive campaign? A reminder that behind the political solution is another one? The soldiers and police are visibly nervous, scanning the streets for snipers°, odd parcels, lurking dangers, and questioning people in the cars that circle for a third time to stare. In a week or two, if nothing happens, the city will begin to relax. But tonight it all seems ominous. All night they will be at work, scraping the glass from the deserted streets.

*People with guns who shoot at individulas from rooftops of other hidden locations.*

[1]"An eye for an eye" refers to a passage from the Old Testament of the Bible. The full quotation is "an eye for an eye, a tooth for a tooth." This statement reflects a philosophy of justice which believes that the punishment should be fitting of the crime.

Source: *Granta* 19, Summer 1986, p. 241.

## COMPREHENSION

Answer the following questions true or false without looking back at the reading.

_____ **1.** The bomb blast in Belfast killed several people.

_____ **2.** The bomb blast created a million pounds of rubble.

_____ **3.** After the bomb blast, the police questioned civilians in cars.

_____ **4.** Nine bombs exploded in six cities.

## ANALYSIS

*IT WORKS!*
*Learning Strategy:*
*Grammar Focus*

This reading includes many "sentence fragments," or sentences that lack either a subject or a verb. Underline all the examples of sentence fragments you can find in the reading.

Compare your findings to a partner's. Did you miss any? Why do you think the author used sentence fragments?

## PREREADING PROJECT

With a partner, locate Beirut on a map. Try to find out what the conflict there is about. Explain the conflict to your class.

**BEIRUT DIARY**

*Robert Fisk*

Monday 1 May

I was sitting on the balcony trying to read by candlelight when I saw flames rise from the sea. An explosion followed. In video-taped news reports of shelling or bombing in Lebanon, the technicians synchronize the sound of a detonation with the visual image of the explosion. In real life you see the fall of shot and hear it afterwards. I have always suspected that a lot of people get killed in wars

☆

because they have spent too much time watching war movies on television. They see an explosion but don't believe it's really happening because they have yet to hear the sound. They don't take cover.

In 1982 I watched Israeli jets bomb houses in Beirut. The planes dived, a small black rugby ball dropped from the wing and an entire apartment block disappeared in grey smoke and crumpled to the ground. Not a sound.

In Jounieh, the missiles were landing only a hundred meters away. The bang came less than a second after the flash. The change in air pressure sent me crawling across the floor into the bathroom. I heard a hiss but it was only my ears, which felt as if they had been boxed repeatedly. Up on the mountainside above the Aquarium a great fire was progressing through the fir trees. In the field where the gardener was cut in half, hundreds of frogs croaked in choral unison.

Source: *Granta* 29, Winter 1989, 235-236.

## ANALYSIS

*IT WORKS!*
*Learning Strategy:*
*Practice*

Address the following questions with a small group of classmates. Have one member of your group read the quotation aloud, then discuss the questions that follow.

**1.** The author of this passage states,

> I have always suspected that a lot of people get killed in wars because they have spent too much time watching war movies on television. They see an explosion but don't believe it's really happening because they have yet to hear the sound. They don't take cover.

Do you think the author is right? In what other ways do you think television has affected our view of war?

**2.** Reread the final sentence of this passage. What contrast is created by this sentence?

## VOCABULARY

*IT WORKS!*
*Learning Strategy:*
*Vocabulary Focus*

The following vocabulary items, taken from the reading, relate to the sounds or activities of war. Write sentences in which you use the words indicated. An extra challenge: do not include any form of the word "be" in your sentences.

**1.** (bang, explosion) _____

_____

**2.** (detonation, bomb) _____

_____

**3.** (shelling) _____

_____

**4.** (hiss, flash) _____

_____

## PREREADING ACTIVITY

Consult an encyclopedia or other reference book about the life of Carl Sandburg. Take notes from your reading. With a partner, write a short report on Sandburg.

*IT WORKS!*
*Learning Strategy:*
*Cooperating*

### Grass

Pile the bodies high at Austerlitz and Waterloo.°
Shovel them under and let me work—
   I am the grass; I cover all.

And pile them high at Gettysburg°
And pile them high at Ypres and Verdun.°
Shovel them under and let me work.
Two years, ten years, and passengers ask the conductor:
   What place is this?
   Where are we now?

   I am the grass.
   Let me work.

                 *Carl Sandburg*

*battle sites in Europe in a war at the beginning of the nineteenth century*

*site of a battle during the U.S. Civil War*

*French battle sites during World War I*

*Carl Sandburg (1878–1967) was an American poet best known for his poems about the city of Chicago.*

## ANALYSIS

With a partner, complete the following. Compare your answers with another pair of students. Did you give the same answers? Discuss the differences.

1. Who is the narrator of this poem? _____

_____

2. Who is "them" in the phrase "pile them high"?

_____

_____

3. In the phrase "the passengers ask the conductor", who are the passengers?

_____

_____

4. Who is the conductor?

_____

_____

**5.** What is the message of this poem, in your opinion?

_____

_____

**6.** Make a list of other battlefields you could add to Sandburg's list.

_____

_____

_____

_____

_____

The photograph below was taken of a portion of the battlefield after the Battle of Gettysburg in July 1863. At right, the cemetary at Normandy, France, where the allies launched the D-Day invasion, June 6, 1944.

*LEARNING STRATEGY*

**Forming Concepts: Making lists of relevant facts in advance can help you understand your readings.**

## PREREADING ACTIVITY

The next two readings concern World War II, and the Japanese-American conflict in particular. What do you know about this conflict? Make a list of all the names and places associated with the Japanese-American conflict in World War II.

# I WAS FAR FROM CONFIDENT

### Zenji Abe[1]

At Pearl Harbor we achieved more than expected. Two days later, the naval air force sank the British battleships *Prince of Wales* and *Repulse* off Malaysia. They were said to be unsinkable, so the central command of the navy began to be overconfident. I was far from confident.

In May 1942 I was assigned to the aircraft carrier *Junyo* to train 18 bomber pilots. My mission was to attack Dutch Harbor in the Aleutian Islands at the same time as the attack on Midway. The commander didn't know anything about planes. Since he remembered the dive bombers' pinpoint strikes in the Indian Ocean, he wanted to use them. But it was not the kind of battle for dive bombers to fight. I lost four of my men. When we returned to Japan, I heard that the carriers *Akagi, Soryu* and *Hiryu* had been sunk by careless mistakes at Midway[2]. Then I realized the war was over.

[1]Mr. Abe was stationed on the flagship Akagi during the attack on Pearl Harbor. He is now 75 years old, and a businessman.

[2]Site of a battle in World War II in June 1942, the Battle of Midway was considered a turning point in the conflict between the U.S. and Japan.

Source: *Time Magazine,* Dec. 2, 1991, p. 50.

*IT WORKS!*
*Learning Strategy:*
*Remembering*

## COMPREHENSION

Answer these questions without looking back at the reading. Fill each blank with one word.

1. At _____ _____ we achieved more than expected.

2. The central command of the _____ began to be overconfident.

3. My _____ was to _____ Dutch Harbor in the Aleutian Islands at the same time as the _____ on Midway.

4. The _____ didn't know anything about planes.

5. When we returned to Japan, I heard that the carriers *Akagi, Soryu* and *Hiryu* had been _____ by careless mistakes at Midway.

## ANALYSIS

Take turns asking a partner the following questions. Make notes of your partner's answers.

1. Why was the commander overconfident?

_____

_____

2. Why did the attack on Dutch Harbor fail?

_____

_____

3. How does the narrator feel now? Underline words or phrases in the passage which tell you this.

_____

_____

## Threads

On September 17, 1991, Liberian rebel leader Charles Taylor agreed to surrender to a multinational peacekeeping force.

# THE MAN FROM HIROSHIMA[1]

*Maurizio Chierici*

I had command of the lead plane, the *Straight Flush*[2] . I flew over Hiroshima for fifteen minutes, studying the clouds covering the target—a bridge between the military zone and the city. Fifteen Japanese fighters were circling beneath me, but they're not made to fly above 29,000 feet where we were to be found. I looked up: cumulus clouds at 10,000, 12,000 meters. The wind was blowing them towards Hiroshima. Perfect weather. I could see the target clearly: the central span of the bridge. I laugh now when I think of the order: "I want only the central arch of the bridge, *only* that, you understand?" Even if I'd guessed that we were carrying something a bit special, the houses, the roads, the city still seemed very far away from our bomb.

I said to myself: This morning's just a big scare for the Japanese.

I transmitted the coded message, but the person who aimed the bomb made an error of 3,000 feet. Towards the city, naturally. But three thousand feet one way or the other wouldn't have made much difference: that's what I thought as I watched it drop. Then the explosion stunned me momentarily. Hiroshima disappeared under a yellow cloud. No one spoke after that. Usually when you return from a mission with everyone still alive, you exchange messages with each other, impressions, congratulations. This time the radios stayed silent; three planes close together and mute. Not for fear of the enemy, but for fear of our own words. Each one of us must have asked forgiveness for the bomb. I'm not religious and I didn't know who to ask forgiveness from, but in that moment I made a promise to myself to oppose all bombs and all wars. Never again that yellow cloud. . .

[1] The man from Hiroshima is Claude Eatherly, who flew the Boeing B-29 described in this reading. His plane carried no bombs. It is Eatherly who is speaking in this passage.

[2] "Straight Flush" is a term referring to a hand in poker. It is the next to highest possible hand (the highest is a royal flush).

Source: *Granta* 22, Autumn, 1987, p 214.

## COMPREHENSION

Answer these questions without looking back at the reading passage. Fill in each blank with one word.

1. I had command of the lead _____, the *Straight Flush*.

2. I flew over _____ for fifteen minutes, studying the clouds covering the _____—a _____ between the military zone and the city.

3. Even if I'd guessed that we were carrying something a bit _____, the houses, the roads, the city still seemed very far away from our _____

4. I said to myself: This morning's just a big _____ for the _____.

5. I transmitted the coded message, but the person who _____the bomb made an _____ of 3,000 feet.

6. I'm not religious and I didn't know who to ask _____ from, but in that moment I made a _____ to myself to oppose all _____ and all _____.

## ANALYSIS

Understanding the following quotations requires you to make *inferences,* that is, to reach a conclusion beyond the information given directly. Look at the following statements made by the narrator of this story, and supply the information you must *infer*. Work with a partner.

1. "I laugh now when I think of the order: 'I want only the central arch of the bridge, *only* that, you understand?'"
   Why did he laugh?

   _____

   _____

2. "I said to myself: This morning's just a big scare for the Japanese."
   Why wasn't it "just a big scare"?

   _____

   _____

3. "Usually when you return from a mission with everyone still alive, you exchange messages with each other, impressions, congratulations. This time the radios stayed silent; three planes close together and mute."
   Why didn't they exchange messages this time?

   _____

   _____

Scanning means selectively reading a piece of writing to find out specific information. Scan the advertisement below to find answers to the questions below. Work quickly. Remember do not read every word.

1. To which war is the special issue dedicated?

_____

2. How long does it take for the special issue to arrive?

_____

3. With which credit cards can you pay?

_____

4. How many pages are in the special issue?

_____

5. How long did the ground war last?

_____

*Newsweek* © 1992

# 43 DAYS OF WAR
# A NEWSWEEK RETROSPECTIVE

**HERE IT IS! OVER 100 STIRRING PAGES. MORE THAN 100 GRIPPING PHOTOS, MANY NEVER BEFORE PUBLISHED. EXCLUSIVE PULL-OUT MAP.**

This is the historical record of America's triumph over Iraq. This special *Newsweek* Commemorative Edition brings you complete photo and news coverage of the many faces of War...

• The Path to War • Behind the Scenes for 43 Days and Nights • Life in the Desert • Bombs Over Baghdad • Saddam on the Ropes • Blitzkrieg: The 100-Hour Ground War • The Final Push • The Iraqis' Hasty Retreat • The Big Five Leaders • Our Soldiers Return • A Tribute to Fallen Heroes • What the War Means For America

**ONLY $3 95
HURRY...ORDER NOW!**

☛ OVER 100 PAGES  ☛ HARD-BACK BINDING
☛ SPECIAL COVER  ☛ EXCLUSIVE PHOTOS
☛ DETAILED FULL COLOR PULL-OUT MAP

**Order toll-free**
**1-800-634-6848**
8:30am - 8pm Eastern Standard Time

**Newsweek**

## 43 DAYS OF WAR
## A NEWSWEEK RETROSPECTIVE

Please rush _____ copies of the special *Newsweek* Commemorative Edition at $3.95 each.

☐ Check  ☐ Money Order

Or charge my: ☐ Visa  ☐ MasterCard  ☐ American Express

Account
Number _____  Exp. Date _____

Signature _____  _____

Name _____

Address _____

City _____ State _____ Zip _____

Mail to: Newsweek Commemorative Edition, P.O. Box 3004, Livingston, NJ 07039-7004

Call Toll-Free 1-800-634-6848 (8:30am - 8pm EST)
Please allow 2-3 week delivery.

## ANALYSIS

Take a vote in your class: How many students would purchase this special issue of *Newsweek*? As a class, discuss the reasons people have for buying or not buying this issue.

## PREREADING HINT

Learning to understand the conventions of punctuation can be helpful in reading dialogue in a short story. Look at the following sentences, from the story "Gregory", then answer the questions that follow.

1. "Why didn't you run away, Gregory?" we asked.
   "It's not bad here," he replied.
   **a.** What does the use of quotation marks (" ") indicate?
   **b.** Explain the order of punctuation marks in the second sentence above.
2. He used to sew on all our buttons, patch our clothes, darn our socks, iron our ties, wash our clothes. . .
   **a.** What does the ellipsis (. . .) indicate?
   **b.** How are the commas used?
3. "Well, one day I stole some cucumbers and melons and watermelons and I took them to her. 'Maria,' I said, 'from now on, I'm going to take care of you.' She started crying and then me, too." What is the difference between using double quotation marks (" ") and single ones (' ')?

**Threads**

President Jean-Betrand Aristide, Haiti's first popularly elected president, was overthrown by a military coup on September 30, 1991.

# GREGORY[1]

## Panos Ioannides

My hand was sweating as I held the pistol. The curve of the trigger was biting against my finger.

Facing me, Gregory trembled.

His whole being was beseeching me, "Don't!"

Only his mouth did not make a sound. His lips were squeezed tight. If it had been me, I would have screamed, shouted, cursed. The soldiers were watching. . .

The day before, during a brief meeting, they had each given their opinions: "It's tough luck, but it has to be done. We've got no choice."

The order from Headquarters was clear: "As soon as Lieutenant Rafel's execution is announced, the hostage Gregory is to be shot and his body must be hanged from a telegraph pole in the main street as an exemplary punishment."

It was not the first time that I had to execute a hostage in this war. I had acquired experience, thanks to Headquarters which had kept entrusting me with these delicate assignments. Gregory's case was precisely the sixth.

The first time, I remember, I vomited. The second time I got sick and had a headache for days. The third time I drank a bottle of rum. The fourth, just two glasses of beer. The fifth time I joked about it, "This little guy, with the big pop-eyes, won't be much of a ghost!"

But why, dammit, when the day came did I have to start thinking that I'm not so tough, after all? The thought had come at exactly the wrong time and spoiled all my disposition to do my duty.

You see, this Gregory was such a miserable little creature, such a puny thing, such a nobody, damn him.

That very morning, although he had heard over the loudspeakers that Rafel had been executed, he believed that we would spare his life because we had been eating together so long.

"Those who eat from the same mess tins and drink from the same water canteen," he said, "remain good friends no matter what."

And a lot more of the same sort of nonsense.

He was a silly fool—we had smelled that out the very first day Headquarters gave him to us. The sentry guarding him had got dead drunk and had dozed off. The rest of us with exit permits had gone from the barracks. When we came back, there was Gregory sitting by the sleeping sentry and thumbing through a magazine.

"Why didn't you run away, Gregory?" we asked, laughing at him, several days later.

And he answered, "Where would I go in this freezing weather? I'm O.K. here."

So we started teasing him.

"You're dead right. The accommodations here are splendid. . ."

"It's not so bad here," he replied. "The barracks where I used to be are like a sieve. The wind blows in from every side. . ."

We asked him about his girl. He smiled.

"Maria is a wonderful person," he told us. "Before I met her she was engaged to a no-good fellow, a pig. He gave her up for another girl. Then nobody in the village wanted to marry Maria. A didn't miss my chance. So what if she is second-hand. Nonsense. Peasant ideas, my friend. She's beautiful and good-hearted. What more could I want? And didn't she load me with watermelons and cucumbers every time I passed by her vegetable garden? Well, one day I stole some cucumbers and melons and watermelons and I took them to her. "Maria," I said, "from now on I'm going to take care of you." She started crying and then me, too. But ever since that day she has given me lots of trouble—jealousy. She wouldn't let me go even to my mother's. Until the day I was recruited, she wouldn't let me go far from her apron strings. But that was just what I wanted. . ."

He used to tell his story over and over, always with the same words, the same commonplace gestures. At the end he would have a good laugh and start gulping from his water jug.

His tongue was always wagging! When he started talking, nothing could stop him. We used to listen and nod our heads, not saying a word. But sometimes, as he was telling us about his mother and family problems, we couldn't help wondering. "Eh, well, these people have the same headaches in their country as we've got."

Strange, isn't it!

Except for his talking too much, Gregory wasn't a bad fellow. He was a marvelous cook. Once he made us some apple tarts, so delicious we licked the platter clean. And he could sew, too. He used to sew on all our buttons, patch our clothes, darn our socks, iron our ties, wash our clothes. . .

How the devil could you kill such a friend?

Even though his name was Gregory and some people on his side had killed one of ours, even though we had left wives and children to go to war against him and his kind—but how can I explain? He was our friend. He actually liked us! A few days before, hadn't he killed with his own bare hands a scorpion that was climbing up my leg? He could have let it send me to hell!

"Thanks, Gregory!" I said then, "Thank God who made you. . ."

When the order came, it was like a thunderbolt. Gregory was to be shot, it said, and hanged from a telegraph pole as an exemplary punishment.

We got together inside the barracks. We sent Gregory to wash some underwear for us.

"It ain't right."

"What is right?"

"Our duty!"

"Shit!"

"If you dare, don't do it! They'll drag you to court-martial and then bang-bang. . ."

Well, of course. The right thing is to save your skin. That's only logical. It's either your skin or his. His, of course, even if it was Gregory, the fellow you've been sharing the same plate with, eating with your fingers, and who was washing your clothes that very minute.

What could I do? That's war. We had seen worse things.

So we set the hour.

We didn't tell him anything when he came back from the washing. He slept peacefully. He snored for the last time. In the morning, he heard the news over the loudspeaker and he saw that we looked gloomy and he began to suspect that something was up. He tried talking to us, but he got no answers and then he stopped talking.

He just stood there and looked at us, stunned and lost. . .

Now, I'll squeeze the trigger. A tiny bullet will rip through his chest. Maybe I'll lose my sleep tonight but in the morning I'll wake up alive.

Gregory seems to guess my thoughts. He puts out his hand and asks, "You're kidding, friend! Aren't you kidding?"

What a jackass! Doesn't he deserve to be cut to pieces? What a thing to ask at such a time. Your heart is about to burst and he's asking if you're kidding. How can a body be kidding about such a thing? Idiot! This is no time for jokes. And you, if you're such a fine friend, why don't you make things easier for us? Help us kill you with fewer qualms? If you would get angry—curse our Virgin, our God—if you'd try to escape it would be much easier for us and for you.

So it is *now*.

Now, Mr. Gregory, you are going to pay for your stupidities wholesale. Because you didn't escape the day the sentry fell asleep; because you didn't escape yesterday when we sent you all alone to the laundry—we did it on purpose, you idiot! Why didn't you let me die from the sting of the scorpion?

So now don't complain. It's all your fault, nitwit.

Eh? What's happening to him now?

Gregory is crying. Tears flood his eyes and trickle down over his cleanshaven cheeks. He is turning his face and pressing his forehead against the wall. His back is shaking as he sobs. His hands cling, rigid and helpless, to the wall.

Now is my best chance, now that he knows there is no other solution and turns his face from us.

I squeeze the trigger.

Gregory jerks. His back stops shaking up and down.

I think I've finished him! How easy it is. . . But suddenly he starts crying out loud, his hands claw at the wall and try to pull it down. He screams, "No, no. . ."

I turn to the others. I expect them to nod, "That's enough."

They nod, "What are you waiting for?"

I squeeze the trigger again.

The bullet smashed into his neck. A thick spray of blood spurts out.

Gregory turns. His eyes are all red. He lunges at me and starts punching me with his fists.

"I hate you, hate you. . ." he screams.

I emptied the barrel. He fell and grabbed my leg as if he wanted to hold on.

He died with a terrible spasm. His mouth was full of blood and so were my boots and socks.

We stood quietly, looking at him.

When we came to, we stooped and picked him up. His hands were frozen and wouldn't let my legs go.

I still have their imprints, red and deep, as if made by a hot knife.

"We will hang him tonight," the men said.

"Tonight or now?" they said.

I turned and looked at them one by one.

"Is that what you all want?" I asked.

They gave me no answer.

"Dig a grave," I said.

Headquarters did not ask for a report the next day or the day after. The top brass were sure that we had obeyed them and had left him swinging from a pole.

They didn't care to know what happened to that Gregory, alive or dead.

[1] This story is based on a true incident that took place during the island of Cyprus's struggle for liberation against the British in the late 1950's.

Translated by Marion Byron Raizis and Catherine Raizis. First published in *The Charioteer, A Review of Modern Greek Literature*. Copyright © 1989 by Panos Ioannides. English language translation © 1989 by Marion Byron and Catherine Raizis. Pella Publishing.

## ANALYSIS

This story may provoke a very strong or emotional response from some readers. It may help to write about your thoughts and feelings before discussing the story in class. In your journal, or on another sheet of paper, write answers to the following questions. Bring your questions to class, and discuss them in small groups.

1. Why was the narrator of the story chosen as the person best suited to kill Gregory?
2. Why didn't Gregory escape when the soldiers gave him the opportunity?
3. Why didn't the soldiers stop the narrator from firing a second shot?
4. The narrator had been ordered to hang Gregory's body from a telegraph pole. What did he do instead? What does this say about his character?
5. What would you have done if you had been in the narrator's place?
6. As mentioned earlier, this story is based on a true occurrence. Why do you think the author chose to write such an unpleasant story?
7. Did you like the story? Why or why not?
8. What message did the author want his readers to understand? What do you think about his message?
9. What does this story say about human behavior? Do you agree with this outlook on human nature?

*IT WORKS!*
*Learning Strategy:*
*Discussing Your*
*Feelings*

# SUMMARY EXERCISES

## Themes

### DISCUSS

Review the chapter and the exercises that accompanied the readings. Identify one idea or reading that affected you the most strongly. Describe it here.

_____

_____

_____

_____

*IT WORKS!*
*Learning Strategy:*
*Asking for*
*Clarification*

Explain your choice to your class, and tell why you were affected by it. Ask your classmates questions about their choices.

## DEBATE

What is an apology? In 1991, the fiftieth anniversary of the bombing of Pearl Harbor, both the Japanese and American governments decided not to apologize for their actions during World War II, although both governments expressed "regret." Should they have apologized?

Address this question in a class debate. Divide your class into two equal parts. Half of the class should argue for an apology, and the other side should argue against one. Each side should get the same amount of time to present its arguments. Use the following list to help you develop your arguments. List the reasons why you support (or disagree with) apologizing. (State each reason as a sentence).

1. _____

2. _____

3. _____

4. _____

(Use an additional piece of paper if you need more space.)

## ROLE-PLAY

With a group of classmates, choose one of the following for a role-play:

- Mr. Abe and Mr. Eatherly meet and discuss the Second World War and their roles in it.
- A reporter talks to the narrator of the story "Gregory," asking him what happened, and how he feels about it now.
- A person living in Beirut, Lebanon, and one living in Belfast, Northern Ireland, meet, and discuss the conflicts in their cities, and how it affects their daily lives.

## WRITE

Are there any wars occurring at the current time? Which ones? With a partner, scan three recent newspapers for stories of war. Together, choose one war that interests you. Read the newspaper stories related to it, and take notes on its history and important events. Write a short (1- or 2-page) report on this conflict. You may wish to add pictures or maps.

## The Cultural Dimension

1. Interview one of your classmates about an important war in which his or her country was involved. Prepare at least five questions to ask. Report on your findings to your class.
2. Interview a U.S. citizen who remembers the Vietnam War. Prepare at least five questions asking about his or her memories of that war and some of the activities that took place during that time.

**Threads**

**Total Budget for the US Department of Defense for 1991—$298.9 billion.**

*U.S. Office of Mangement & Budget*

## Self-Evaluation Questionnaire

Make a list of new words and ideas you learned from this chapter.

1. _____
2. _____
3. _____
4. _____
5. _____
6. _____
7. _____
8. _____
9. _____
10. _____

As you did in previous chapters, think about the goals you set at the beginning of the chapter. How well did you perform? Review your progress, then rate yourself on how you think you did in each of the following areas for this chapter. Give yourself the following ratings:

**5 excellent  4 good  3 average  2 fair  1 poor**

|  | RATING |
| --- | --- |
| **A.** Improved reading speed | _____ |
| **B.** Understood main ideas | _____ |
| **C.** Increased vocabulary understanding | _____ |
| **D.** Learned more about the topic of the chapter | _____ |
| **E.** Developed more understanding of style and grammar | _____ |

Compare your ratings with the objectives you set on the first page of this chapter.

# Eco-Politics

# PLANNING & GOALS

As you did in earlier chapters, list in order of priority (with 1 as 'most important') the goals that are important to you in this chapter.

| GOAL | RANK |
|---|---|
| **A.** To increase reading speed | ____ |
| **B.** To increase comprehension of main ideas | ____ |
| **C.** To improve vocabulary understanding | ____ |
| **D.** To learn more about the information in thischapter | ____ |
| **E.** To improve understanding of style and grammar | ____ |

# LOOKING AHEAD

"Eco-politics" is the combination of politics with ecological concerns. As the world population grows, and resources are strained, the joining of political concerns to ecological ones becomes a focus in world policy. Local environmental issues become global matters.

Here is a list of some of the readings included in this chapter on the world's ecological policy.

"The World's Endangered Mammals," by M. E. Sokolik

"Saving the Planet," by Alan B. Durning

"Fire and Ice," a poem by Robert Frost

"Paradise Lost: The Ravaged Rainforest," by Ellen Hosmer

*IT WORKS!*
*Learning Strategy:*
*Guessing*

Thinking about these titles, discuss the following questions with a partner:

1. What do you think the world's biggest ecological concern is today?
2. Have you or your family taken any steps to help improve the environment? What are they?
3. Look ahead at the graphic material included in this chapter. What does it tell you about the subject matter?
4. What would you like to know about this topic?

## Try a New Strategy

Graphic materials such as photographs can help your understanding of reading material. Locate books or magazines that portray various endangered animals or environments.

*IT WORKS!*
*Learning Strategy:*
*Taking Notes*

## LISTENING

Check the newspaper or the magazine *TV Guide* to locate a nature program, such as "National Geographic," or a program on public television, or the cable television channel called "The Discovery Channel." Choose one program you would like to watch, and watch it either on your own or with a classmate. Then answer the following questions.

**A.** On your own, use the following spaces to take notes as you watch the program you selected.

**1.** The name of the program I watched:

_____

**2.** What animal(s) or ecological issue was treated by the program?

_____

**3.** Describe the story treated by the program.

_____

_____

_____

_____

**4.** List any new vocabulary items you learned from the program.

_____

_____

_____

**B.** Form a group with others who watched a different program than you did.

**1.** Describe to your partners your answer for question 3. Try to recall all the details you can.

_____

_____

_____

_____

_____

_____

_____

## Threads

Radioactivity from the Chernobyl nuclear reactor contaminated food products across northern Europe in 1986.

**Overcoming Limitations: Using words with similar meanings, as well as gestures, can help you get your message across.**

**2.** Teach your partners the meanings of any new words you listed in question 4 above. When teaching the words, use synonyms, gestures, pictures, anything you need to get the meaning across.

*IT WORKS!*
*Learning Strategy:*
*Getting the Idea*

## PREREADING ACTIVITY

Read the first paragraph of the following reading. What do you think the point of view of the author is, based on this paragraph?

# PARADISE LOST:
# THE RAVAGED RAIN FOREST

*Ellen Hosmer*

Tropical forests are located in some 70 countries, but about 80 percent are in Bolivia, Brazil, Colombia, Gabon, Indonesia, Malaysia, Peru, Venezuela, and Zaire. The rain forests are home to nearly half of all the plants, animals, and insects in the world. Notes the World Wildlife Fund, "More species of fish live in the Amazon River than in the entire Atlantic Ocean."

Tropical plants produce chocolate, nuts, tannins[1], fruits, gums, coffee, waxes, wood and wood products, rubber and petroleum substitutes, and ingredients found in toothpaste, pesticides, fibers, and dyes.

In addition, several medical wonders of the twentieth century have come from plants found only in rain forests. These plants have been used to treat high blood pressure, Hodgkin's disease,[2] multiple sclerosis,[3] and Parkinson's disease.[4] The tiny periwinkle flower from the rain forest in madagascar, for example, is key to a drug that has been successfully used to treat lymphocytic leukemia[5]. And rain forests may hold the answer to treatment for several types of cancer. A study of the Costa Rican rain forest found that 15 percent of the plants studied had potential as anti-cancer agents.

"We are destroying the biological heritage that developed over billions of years and doing it in the matter of a few human generations," says Paul Ehrlich of Stanford University. "Our descendants, if any, will be very much the poorer for it."

[1]Tannic acid, a yellow substance used in tanning and dying.
[2]A type of cancer.
[3]A desease of the central nervous system.
[4]A disease affecting older people, causing tremors and rigid muscles.
[5]Another type of cancer.

Source: Excerpted from the *Multinational Monitor*, June 1987, p. 6.

## COMPREHENSION

Answer the following questions true or false without looking back at the reading passage.

_____ 1. 80 percent of tropical forests are located in Bolivia, Brazil, Colombia, Gabon, Indonesia, Malaysia, Peru, Venezuela, and Zaire.

_____ 2. Rain forests are home to nearly one-quarter of all the plants, animals, and insects in the world.

_____ 3. More species of fish live in the Amazon River than in the entire Atlantic Ocean.

_____ 4. The periwinkle flower from the rain forest in Madagascar is key to a drug that has been successfully used to treat lymphocytic leukemia.

_____ 5. A study of the Costa Rican rain forest found that 75 percent of the plants there were potential anti-cancer agents.

## ANALYSIS

"We are destroying the biological heritage that developed over billions of years and doing it in the matter of a few human generations," says Paul Ehrlich of Stanford University. "Our descendants, if any, will be very much the poorer for it." List the ways that you think the descendants will be "poorer" because of the loss of the rain forests.

_____

_____

_____

_____

_____

_____

_____

_____

_____

_____

## Threads

In 1989, the tanker Exxon Valdez released 35,000 tons of oil into Prince William Sound, Alaska.

## ANALYSIS

What makes the cartoon on page 93 humorous is the impossibility of controls having the effect shown in the picture. What is that effect? What does this say about the effectiveness of local controls and the need for global regulation? Discuss these questions with your class.

"They have very strict anti-pollution laws in this state."

## PREREADING HINT

Learning to discriminate words quickly is an important part of improving reading speed. The key words in the far left column are taken from the readings in this chapter. Scan each line, and circle each occurrence of the word. Work quickly.

Starting time: _____

| | | | | |
|---|---|---|---|---|
| 1. *ecology* | economy | ecology | economics | biology |
| 2. *leopard* | leopard | lemur | leotard | leopard |
| 3. *habitat* | habit | habitant | habitat | habits |
| 4. *pollution* | solution | pollution | pollen | dilution |
| 5. *forests* | frets | feet | fences | forests |
| 6. *genetics* | frenetic | genetics | genes | gentler |
| 7. *extinct* | extinct | excuse | extra | extinct |
| 8. *monkey* | money | monkey | many | donkey |
| 9. *hunting* | punting | hanging | lunging | hunting |
| 10. *endanger* | dangers | endanger | enrage | derange |

Finishing time: _____

## THE WORLD'S ENDANGERED MAMMALS

*M. E. Sokolik*

### I. Great Cats

A. Jaguar (*Panthera onca*): The jaguar's natural range once extended from the southwest of the U.S. to nearly the southern most tip of South America. However, hunting for its pelt and the destruction of its habitat has brought the jaguar to near extinction.

*The biological name is included in parentheses.*

B. Leopard: The most common type of African leopard (*Panthera pardus*) is not endangered, only threatened. However, the clouded leopard (*Neofelis nebulosa*), found in south central Asia, and the snow leopard (*Panthera uncia*), found in the Himalayan mountains of Asia, are endangered.

C. Cheetah (*Acinonyx jubatus*): The cheetah population which ranges from Africa to India is particularly fragile because there is very little genetic diversity in the cats that still exist. Hunting and changes in the environment also threaten the cheetah.

D. Tiger (*Panthera tigris*): Hunting and destruction of the natural habitat of the tiger have forced it to near extinction.

## II. Apes and Monkeys

A. Monkeys: Many types of monkeys, especially those from South and Central America, are endangered. The howler monkey (*Alouatta palliata*) and the spider monkey (*Ateles geoffroyi*) come from this area, and face extinction. The colobus (*Colobus kirki*) in Africa was hunted for its fur, and now faces habitat destruction as well. All monkeys have been threatened by collection as pets.

B. Gibbon (*Hylobates,* all species): Habitat destruction threatens this primitive ape.

C. Gorilla (*Gorilla gorilla*): The sale of baby gorillas has contributed to the depletion of the gorilla population in the world. Gorillas have also been a food source, which led to excessive hunting. Souvenir seekers also seek gorilla hands to use as ashtrays.[1]

D. Orangutan (*Pongo pygmaeus*): This ape was once found all over southern Asia, but it is now located only in parts of the islands of Sumatra and Borneo. Collecting and habitat destruction have contributed to the threat of this animal's extinction, but a low birth-rate and susceptibility to many diseases have added to the orangutan's problems as well.

E. African chimpanzee (*Pan troglodytes*): African chimpanzees are classified as endangered, but the approximately 600 chimps in the U.S. are listed only as threatened.

## III. Sea Mammals

A. Dugong (*Dugong dugon*): Also called the sea cow, this mammal lives in shallow waters along the coasts of the western Pacific Ocean. Since the dugong is a mild-mannered animal, it is easy to catch, and is prized for its meat and hide, which makes fine leather. Although the dugong is protected, it is difficult to monitor hunting at sea.

B. Whales (many species): Since 1986, the International Whaling Commission has prohibited almost all whaling, although some fishing by native groups, such as the Inuit in Alaska, is allowed. Some are allowed to be taken for research, although this practice is controversial. Many different species of whales, including the humpback (*Megaptera novaeangliae*), the bowhead (*Balaena mysticetus*), and the gray whale (*Eschrichtius robustus*), are endangered.

## IV. Others

A. Giant panda (*Ailuropoda melanoleuca*): The panda is found only in the western mountains of China, and eats only bamboo shoots; these two factors contribute to its endangerment. Zoos have collected pandas to try to improve their breeding rate, but this practice has probably contributed to their depletion

as well. Although the panda is one of the most popular animals in the world, and is protected by the Chinese government by strict laws, it is still in serious danger of extinction.

B. Rhinoceros: The Asian species, the black rhinoceros (*Diceros bicornis*) and the northern white rhinocerous (*Ceratotherium simum cottoni*), are both seriously endangered, although nearly all species of rhinoceros face extinction. The main problem is the poaching of these animals for their horns, which are valued for their medicinal properties by the Chinese. The horns are also used for knife and sword handles by Arabs. Both of these practices have probably contributed to the threats to the Asian species of rhino.

[1]The film "Gorillas in the Mist" portrays well the plight of the gorilla and its struggle for survival. This film can be found on videocassette at most video rental stores.

## COMPREHENSION

Answer these questions without looking back at the reading.

1. What was once the panther's natural range?
   a. from the U.S. to South America
   b. the African continent
   c. Asia
   d. India
2. The leopard is found in which area?
   a. the U.S.
   b. Asia
   c. Africa
   d. South America
3. What is the primary reason the cheetah population is threatened?
   a. destruction of the environment
   b. overpopulation of cats
   c. lack of genetic diversity
   d. hunting practices
4. All monkeys and apes are threatened by one of the following factors:
   a. hunting for food
   b. hunting for fur
   c. habitat destruction
   d. collection for zoos
5. A dugong is a type of
   a. ape
   b. bird
   c. mammal
   d. fish
6. One part of the rhinocerous makes it particularly attractive to hunters. It is the
   a. skin for leather
   b. horn for medicine
   c. meat for food
   d. heads for trophies

*IT WORKS!*
*Learning Strategy:*
*Associating*

## ANALYSIS

1. Fill in the table below by writing in the name of individual animals that are threatened by the particular factors listed.

| HUNTING | HABITAT DESTRUCTION | COLLECTING | GENETIC PROBLEMS | LOW BIRTH-RATE |
|---------|---------------------|------------|------------------|----------------|
| _____ | _____ | _____ | _____ | _____ |
| _____ | _____ | _____ | _____ | _____ |
| _____ | _____ | _____ | _____ | _____ |
| _____ | _____ | _____ | _____ | _____ |
| _____ | _____ | _____ | | |

Compare your answers with those of a classmate. Then discuss the following questions.

2. What is the one factor that seems to threaten the survival of nearly all endangered or threatened species? What do you think could be done to improve this situation?

3. Why is extinction of any animal a problem, either to that species or others?

## PREREADING ACTIVITY

Draw a word map, using the word "environment," placed in the box below. If you do not remember how to do a word map, look back at page 00.

environment

# SAVING THE PLANET

*Alan B. During*

1    Environmental quality is not a luxury. Those who live beyond the borders of the world's industrial economy subsist on nature's surplus—soil fertility for food, stable hydrological cycles for water, and forests for fuel. Environmental degradation, consequently, has direct, tangible results: hunger, thirst, and fuel scarcity. No line can be drawn between economic development and environmental protection.

2    The world's largest rain forest envelops the thousand tributaries of the Amazon River, forming a great fan that covers northern Brazil and spreads into Venezuela, Colombia, Ecuador, Peru, and Bolivia. The traditional inhabitants of this great basin include dozens of tribes of Indians and 300,000 rubber tappers, a guild of workers who earn their living by tapping the rubber trees spread through the region.

3    Since the 1960s, a series of powerful economic and political forces has brought waves of landless peasants and wealthy land-speculators into the jungles, where they have driven the rubber tappers out—sometimes at gunpoint. The newcomers proceed to clear-cut the woodlands and burn the fallen logs, causing unprecedented destruction and enormous releases of air pollution. In 1987 alone, an area almost the size of Maine° went up in smoke.

4    In the late 1970s, a union of 30,000 rubber tappers from the remote Brazilian state of Acre decided to draw the line. At first, their tactics were simple and direct: Where the chain saws were working, men, women, and children would peacefully occupy the forest, putting their bodies in the path of destruction. This non-violent method was met with violent reprisals that continue today. Last December, two gunmen ambushed Francisco Mendes Filho, national leader of the rubber tappers union, killing him instantly.

*Also about the same size as Austria or Panama—approximately 33,000 square miles (85,800 square kilometers).*

5    The price of their struggle has been high, but the rubber tappers have made modest gains. Bolstered by an unprecedented alliance with indigenous tribes and the scattered beginnings of a nationwide rubber tappers' movement, the union has demanded an end to the destruction of the land—and an end to violence against their members. They have helped reshape World Bank and Inter-American Development Bank lending policy by showing that, over the long run, natural-rubber production is more profitable and creates more employment per hectare than cattle ranching or farming. With help from international environmental groups, the union has called on the Brazilian government to set off large "extractive reserves" where tappers can carry on their way of life in perpetuity. And among the rubber trees of the Amazon forest, they have built community schools and health posts.

6    Across the Pacific, Borneo's Dayak tribe has been less fortunate. The island's dense woodlands are a foundation of Malaysia's foreign-exchange/export strategy, providing the country with most of its billion-dollar annual hardwood trade. The Dayaks, however, want it lumbered only on a sustainable basis and have battled timber contractors by constructing roadblocks and appealing to European consumers to boycott Malaysian hardwoods. To date, government policies have stymied their efforts. The official attitude is summed up by state Minister of the Environment Datuk James Wong, himself a timber tycoon: "There is too much sympathy for the Dayaks. Their swidden lifestyle must be stamped out."

7    The well-organized Kuna Indians of Panama, on the other hand, have been able to establish their homeland as a biological reserve, putting it off-limits to the settlers and cattle ranchers who,

predictably, followed a new access road. In 1980 then-President Omar Torrijos demanded, "Why do you Kuna need so much land? You don't do anything with it. . . . If anyone else so much as cuts down a single tree, you shout and scream."

8    A local leader responded, "If I go to Panama City and stand in front of a pharmacy and, because I need medicine, pick up a rock and break the window, you would take me away and put me in jail. For me, the forest is my pharmacy. If

I have sores on my legs, I go to the forest and get the medicine I need to cure them. The forest is also a great refrigerator. It keeps the food I need fresh. . . . So we Kuna need the forest, and we use it and we take much from it. But we can take what we need without having to destroy everything, as your people do."

The world's most acclaimed community forest movement, Chipko, shows how grass-roots action to defend a resource can grow into far more. Born in the Garhwal hills of Uttar Pradesh, India, Chipko first drew fame for its sheer courage. In March 1973, as a timber company headed for the woods above one impoverished village, desperate local men, women, and children rushed ahead of them to *chipko* (literally, "hug" or "cling to") the trees, daring the loggers to let the axes fall on their backs.

Since its initial success, the movement has deepened its ecological understanding and, in the words of movement follower Vandana Shiva, "widened from embracing trees to embracing mountains and waters." In 1987, for example, activists formed a seven-month blockade at a limestone quarry that was recklessly destroying the ecosystem of an entire valley. Chipko has gone beyond resource protection to ecological management, restoration, and what members call "eco-development." The women who first guarded trees against loggers now plant trees, build soil-retention walls, and prepare village forestry plants.

Grass-roots groups organize most readily to defend their resource base against the incursion of outsiders, but in the right circumstances they may organize to reverse deterioration driven by forces internal to the community.

12    As Kenya's forests shrink, thousands of women's groups, youth clubs, and *harambee* (let's pull together) societies have mounted local tree planting drives. The National Council of Women of Kenya inaugurated its Greenbelt Movement in 1977, calling on women's groups across the country to turn open spaces, school grounds, and roadsides into forests. More than a million trees in 1,000 greenbelts are now straining skyward, 20,000 mini-greenbelts have taken root, and 670 community tree nurseries are in place. Meanwhile, Kenya's largest women's development network, Maendeleo Ya Wanawake, with its 10,000 member groups, initiated a campaign in 1985 to construct improved, wood-saving cookstoves.

13    An African federation popularly known as Naam is among the most successful of the world's grassroots movements at mobilizing people to protect and restore natural resources in an area degraded from overuse. Building on pre-colonial self-help traditions, Naam taps vast stores of peasant knowledge, creativity, and energy to loosen the grip of poverty and ecological deterioration in the drought-prone Sahel region of West Africa. With origins in Burkina Faso, it now spills over under different names into Mauritania, Senegal, Mali, Niger, and Togo.

14    Each year during the dry season, thousands of Naam villages undertake projects chosen designed with minimal assistance from outsiders. Along with five neighboring communities, for example, the settlement of Sommiaga built a large dam and a series of check dams to trap drinking and irrigation water and to slow soil erosion. Villagers piled caged rocks by hand to form a dam four meters high

15 and 180 meters long. Meanwhile, hundreds of Naam farmers have adopted a simple technique of soil and water conservation developed by Oxfam-UK, in which stones are piled in low rows along the contour to hold back the runoff from torrential rains. While halting soil loss, these *diguetes* increase crop yields dramatically.

Source: Excerpted from *The Progressive*, April 1989, as it appeared in the *UTNE Reader*, July/August 1989, pp. 44-45.

## ANALYSIS

Write a one-sentence summary of the following paragraphs (given by number).

Paragraph 1.

_____

_____

Paragraph 3.

_____

_____

Paragraph 6.

_____

_____

Paragraph 9.

_____

_____

Paragraph 12.

_____

_____

Paragraph 14.

_____

# VOCABULARY

Look at the following phrases, taken from the reading. Choose a synonym from the list below to substitute for the italicized words or phrases. The first is done for you.

*IT WORKS!*
*Learning Strategy:*
*Vocabulary Focus*

| | | | | |
|---|---|---|---|---|
| damage | material | encloses | streams | flooding |
| curve | growth areas | native | attacked | supported |
| forever | fundamental | embargo | frustrated | |

1. Environmental *degradation,* consequently, has direct, *tangible* results.

   _____*material*_____        _____*damage*_____

2. The world's largest rain forest *envelops* the thousand *tributaries* of the Amazon River.

   _____        _____

3. Last December, two gunmen *ambushed* Francisco Mendes Filho, national leader of the rubber tappers union.

   _____

4. *Bolstered* by an unprecedented alliance with *indigenous* tribes, the union has demanded an end to the destruction.

   _____        _____

5. Tappers can carry on their way of life *in perpetuity.*

   _____

6. The Dayaks, have battled timber contractors by appealing to European consumers to *boycott* Malaysian hardwoods.

   _____

7. To date, government policies have *stymied* their efforts.

   _____

8. Chipko, shows how *grass-roots* action to defend a resource can grow into far more.

   _____

9. More than a million trees in 1,000 *greenbelts* are now straining skyward.

   _____

10. Stones are piled in low rows along the *contour* to hold back the runoff from *torrential* rains.

    _____        _____

## PREREADING ACTIVITY

In an encyclopedia or other reference book, look up information on the life of Robert Frost. Take notes, and write a short biography using the notes. Try to find a picture of the poet, too.

### Fire and Ice

Some say the world will end in fire,
Some say in ice.
From what I've tasted of desire
I hold with those who favor fire.
But if it had to perish twice,
I think I know enough of hate
To say that for destruction ice
Is also great
And would suffice.

*Robert Frost*

*Robert Frost
(1874-1963)
a poet from the north-
eastern U.S. This poem
was written in 1923,
and is one of his most
famous.*

## ANALYSIS

1. In one or two words, summarize the theme of this poem.
2. What emotions are associated with fire? With ice?
3. Do you think the world will end in ice or in fire (or neither)? Why? In modern terms, what could these images refer to? (For example, "fire" could be global warming.)

# SUMMARY EXERCISES

## Themes

## DISCUSS

*IT WORKS!
Learning Strategy:
Selecting the Topic*

Write one question you would like to ask your class concerning the themes presented in this chapter.

_____

_____

In a class discussion, ask a classmate your question. Make notes of the questions and answers presented in your class discussion.

## DEBATE

From the class discussion, in a group of four or more students, develop a topic for debate. Divide your group into two equal parts. Half of your group should argue for one side of the issue you chose, and the other side should argue for the other. Use the following outline to help you develop your arguments.

Topic:

_____

_____

State your side's opinion in one sentence.

_____

What are the reasons you believe this? Again, state each reason as a sentence.

_____

_____

_____

_____

_____

_____

_____

(Use an additional piece of paper if you need more space.) Present your debate to the class. Each side should get the same amount of time to present its arguments.

Automobile emissions have helped to create a major smog problem in Los Angeles, California.

## ROLE-PLAY

Imagine you and four other students have been appointed by your mayor to lead your city's environmental improvement efforts. Acting as the committee, decide the following:

What are the five worst environmental problems your community faces today?

1. _____
2. _____
3. _____
4. _____
5. _____

What specific proposals do you have to improve those problems? Hold a meeting of the committee to make proposals. (You may want to think about this on your own before meeting with your committee.)

## WRITE

Choose one of the following topics to write about.

1. Research an environmental agency, such as Greenpeace. What kind of work do they do? Who is involved with doing that work? Write a short report explaining what you found out about the organization. Summarize your report orally for your class.
2. Look in a current news magazine, such as *Time* or *Newsweek*, or a newspaper for a story on ecology. Read the story, and summarize it in writing. Report on the story to your class.

## The Cultural Dimension

1. Interview a classmate on the ecological problems that exist in his or her home country. Prepare at least five questions to ask about this topic. Report on your interview to the class.
2. Interview a U.S. citizen about his or her opinion of the ecological problems of the U.S. Prepare at least five questions about this topic. Tape record your interview or take detailed notes. Write a report on the results of your interview.

*IT WORKS!*
*Learning Strategy:*
*Developing Cultural*
*Understanding*

## Self-Evalution Questionnaire

Make a list of new things you learned from this chapter.

1. _____

2. _____

3. _____

4. _____

5. _____

6. _____

7. _____

8. _____

9. _____

10. _____

As you did in previous chapters, think about the goals you set at the beginning of the chapter. How well did you perform? Review your progress, then rate yourself in each of the following areas for this chapter. Give yourself the following ratings:

**5 excellent  4 good  3 average  2 fair  1 poor**

|  | RATING |
|---|---|
| **A.** Improved reading speed | _____ |
| **B.** Understood main ideas | _____ |
| **C.** Increased vocabulary understanding | _____ |
| **D.** Learned more about the topic of the chapter | _____ |
| **E.** Developed more understanding of style and grammar | _____ |

Compare your ratings with the objectives you set on the first page of this chapter.

# Travel

# PLANNING & GOALS

As you have done in earlier chapters, list in order of priority (with 1 as 'most important') the objectives that are important to you.

*IT WORKS!*
*Learning Strategy:*
*Setting Goals*

| GOAL | RANK |
|---|---|
| **A.** To increase reading speed | _____ |
| **B.** To increase comprehension of main ideas | _____ |
| **C.** To improve vocabulary understanding | _____ |
| **D.** To learn more about the information in this chapter | _____ |
| **E.** To improve understanding of style and grammar | _____ |

# LOOKING AHEAD

Advances in technology have allowed people to move from place to place as never before. This ease of travel has caused groups of people, previously unknown to each other, to come into contact. This has many benefits, but it has its disadvantages as well.

Here are some of the readings included in this chapter, which discuss the subject of world travel.

"Watching the Rain in Galicia," by Gabriel García Márquez

"A Small Place," by Jamaica Kincaid

"Observations After Landfall," by Christopher Columbus

"Events in the Skies," by Doris Lessing

Discuss the following questions with a partner.

1. Which titles interest you the most?
2. Which authors are you familiar with? What do you know about them?
3. Do you enjoy reading about travel?
4. Look ahead at the graphic material included in this chapter. What does it tell you about the subject matter?

## PREREADING HINT

Effective readers do not read every word. In this exercise, you will see that you can understand a reading passage even if some of the words are missing. Reading in this way will help improve your reading speed.

Read the following passage. (Do NOT write the missing words in the blanks.) Then answer the questions that follow.

### ARCTIC DREAMS

*Barry Lopez*

Over the past twenty years, some of the focus of academic geography has shifted away from descriptions of the land and focused instead on landscapes that exist in the human mind. The extent and complexity _____ these geographical images, called mental maps, _____ wonderful. An urban resident, _____ example, sees himself situated in urban _____ with specific reference to certain stores,_____ parking _____, and public transportation stations. He_____ one street or building more importance than another as a place for meetings with friends. He knows which routes between certain points safest and how to get to a certain restaurant even though he doesn't know the of any of the streets on the _____.

From *Arctic Dreams*, 1986 by Barry Lopez, New York, MacMillan Pub. Co.

Answer the following questions true or false.

_____ **1.** Modern geography is now interested in something known as "mental maps."

_____ **2.** Many urban residents know how to get places without knowing street names.

_____ **3.** The city dweller frequently gets lost.

## Try a New Strategy

Research has shown that being optimistic, that is, concentrating on how much you already know (instead of how much you do not know) can help you make progress. At this point, take time to make a list of all the reading strategies and skills you have learned so far. Include strategies you have learned on your own, as well as from this textbook.

### LEARNING STRATEGY

**Personalizing: Working with friends who are native English speakers helps you personalize the language and understand it in a natural setting.**

## LISTENING

Ask an English-speaking friend to tape-record a description of his or her favorite travel destination. (Ask that the description not be any longer than five minutes.) Listen to the tape, and transcribe, that is, copy word for word, your friend's description. Bring your transcription to class, and summarize it for a partner.

## *LEARNING STRATEGY*

**Remembering New Material: Classifying words into meaningful groups helps you remember them more clearly.**

The following list outlines things you should do if you are going to take a long trip. Try to remember one meaningful *noun* from each item on the list which will help you remember the entire item. You may want to underline or highlight that noun, if you think it will help.

Traveler's Checklist

| I. | THINGS TO DO |
|----|--------------|
| A. | Ask the post office to hold your mail, or ask a friend to collect it |
| B. | Arrange for someone to take care of your pets |
| C. | Suspend your newspaper subscription |
| D. | Confirm your travel times with the travel agent |
| E. | Put identification in and on your luggage |
| F. | Lock all windows and doors |

| II. | THINGS TO BRING |
|-----|-----------------|
| A. | Tickets |
| B. | Passport, visa, and health certificates |
| C. | Medical information and prescriptions |
| D. | Travelers checks, cash, or credit cards |
| E. | Names and addresses in case of emergency |
| F. | Names and addresses of places where you'll stay |
| G. | Addresses of friends and family you'll write to |

## COMPREHENSION

**A.** Without looking back at the list, write down everything you can remember it instructed you to do.

1. _____
2. _____
3. _____
4. _____
5. _____
6. _____
7. _____
8. _____
9. _____
10. _____
11. _____
12. _____
13. _____

Now check your list against the original. How many did you remember accurately?

**B.** Now make a list of things you could add to the original list.

1. _____
2. _____
3. _____
4. _____
5. _____
6. _____
7. _____
8. _____
9. _____
10. _____

## PREREADING QUESTION

How do you feel about being a tourist? The next two readings discuss differing attitudes towards being a tourist. As you read these articles, make notes about why each author likes or dislikes being a tourist.

*IT WORKS!*
*Learning Strategy:*
*Taking Notes*

## WATCHING THE RAIN IN GALICIA

### Gabriel García Márquez[1]

I don't know where the shame of being a tourist comes from. I've heard many friends in full touristic swing say that they don't want to mix with tourists, not realizing that even though they don't mix with them, they are just as much tourists as the others. When I visit a place and haven't enough time to get to know it more than superficially, I unashamedly assume my role as tourist. I like to join those lightning tours in which the guides explain everything you see out of the window—"On your right and left, ladies and gentlemen. . ."—one of the reasons being that then I know once and for all everything I needn't bother to see when I go out later to explore the place on my own.

[1] Gabriel García Márquez was born in the South American country of Colombia in 1928. He was the oldest of 16 children. He has spent most of his life in Mexico and Europe. He has written many popular novels, which have been translated into more than 30 languages. These novels include *One Hundred Years of Solitude*, *The Autumn of the Patriarch*, and *Chronicle of a Death Foretold*.

Source: *Granta* 10, 1984, p. 10 (Translated from the Spanish by Margaret Costa).

*IT WORKS!*
*Learning Strategy:*
*Discuss Your Feelings*

## ANALYSIS

Discuss the following questions with your class, or in a small group: Have you ever taken a guided tour? Describe what it was like. Would you do it again?

## A SMALL PLACE

### Jamaica Kincaid[1]

*ordinaryness, plainness*

An ugly thing, that is what you become when you become a tourist, an ugly, empty thing, a stupid thing, a piece of rubbish pausing here and there to gaze at this and taste that, and it will never occur to you that the people who inhabit the place in which you have just paused cannot stand you, that behind their closed doors they laugh at your strangeness (you do not look the way they look); the physical sight of you does not please them; you have bad manners (it is their custom to eat their food with their hands; you try eating their way, you look silly; you try eating the way you always eat, you look silly); they do not like the way you speak (you have an accent); they collapse helpless from laughter, mimicking the way they imagine you must look at you carry out some everyday bodily function. They do not like you. *They do not like me!* That thought never actually occurs to you. Still you feel a little uneasy. Still, you feel a little foolish. Still, you feel a little out of place. But the banality° of your own life is very real to you; it drove you to this extreme, spending your days and your nights in the company of people who despise you, people you do not like really, people you would not want to have as your actual neighbour.

[1] Jamaica Kincaid is a Caribbean writer from the island of Antigua. She now lives in the U.S., but continues to write about the island experience. In addition to *A Small Place*, from which this reading was taken, she has also written *Annie John* and *At the Bottom of the River*.

Source: Excerpt from *A Small Place*, New York: Farrar, Straus & Giroux, p.17.

## ANALYSIS

Compare this reading to García Márquez's. With a partner, complete the following information:

Write a one sentence summary of each author's point of view.

Kincaid: _____

García Márquez: _____

What reasons does each give for that point of view?

**Kincaid**                                **García-Márquez**

_____        _____

_____        _____

_____        _____

Whose point of view do you agree with more? Why?

_____

_____

## READING HINT: READING NUMBERS

Below are tables that show distances between some of the world's major cities and the weather in those cities. Use these tables to answer the questions that follow them.

Air Distances in Miles (approximate) Between Major World Cities

| STARTING POINT: | SAN FRANCISCO INTERNATIONAL AIRPORT | CHICAGO O'HARE AIRPORT | NEW YORK KENNEDY AIRPORT |
|---|---|---|---|
| **Destination** | **Distance** | | |
| Bangkok | 7930 | 8570 | 8670 |
| Buenos Aires | 6250 | 5580 | 5280 |
| Cairo | 7440 | 6120 | 5600 |
| Hong Kong | 6900 | 7800 | 8060 |
| London | 5370 | 3960 | 3440 |
| Madrid | 5800 | 4190 | 3600 |
| Mexico City | 1890 | 1690 | 2090 |
| Moscow | 5890 | 4990 | 4680 |
| Paris | 5580 | 4150 | 3640 |
| Rio de Janeiro | 6620 | 5290 | 4810 |
| Rome | 6260 | 4820 | 4290 |
| Singapore | 8450 | 9380 | 9540 |
| Tokyo | 5150 | 6310 | 6050 |

*Adapted from Hammond Travel Mate, Newsweek, Inc.*

**A.** Choose the airport in the city nearest to your location.

   **1.** Which destination is nearest? _____

   **2.** Which destination is farthest? _____

   **3.** What city would you like to visit? _____

   **4.** What is its distance from the nearest airport? _____

**B.** Use all airports and destinations for the following questions.

   **5.** What is the longest trip you can take? From _____ to _____ is _____ miles.

   **6.** What is the shortest: from _____ to _____ is _____ miles.

For the next table, four figures are given for each month. The first pair (for example, 78/25) is the average daily high and low temperatures in Fahrenheit, the second pair is in Celsius. The number to the right of the temperatures is the average number of days of rain.

Destination City Weather

| DESTINATION | | JANUARY | | APRIL | | JULY | | OCTOBER | |
|---|---|---|---|---|---|---|---|---|---|
| Bangkok | F: | 89/68 | 1 | 95/77 | 3 | 90/76 | 13 | 88/75 | 14 |
| | C: | 32/20 | | 35/25 | | 32/24 | | 31/24 | |
| Buenos Aires | F: | 85/63 | 7 | 72/53 | 8 | 57/42 | 8 | 69/50 | 9 |
| | C: | 29/17 | | 22/12 | | 14/6 | | 21/10 | |
| Cairo | F: | 65/47 | 1 | 83/57 | 1 | 96/70 | 0 | 86/65 | 1 |
| | C: | 18/8 | | 28/14 | | 36/21 | | 30/18 | |
| Hong Kong | F: | 64/56 | 4 | 75/67 | 8 | 87/78 | 17 | 81/73 | 6 |
| | C: | 18/13 | | 24/19 | | 31/26 | | 27/23 | |
| London | F: | 44/35 | 17 | 56/40 | 14 | 73/55 | 13 | 58/44 | 14 |
| | C: | 7/2 | | 13/4 | | 23/13 | | 14/7 | |
| Madrid | F: | 47/33 | 9 | 64/44 | 9 | 87/62 | 3 | 66/48 | 8 |
| | C: | 8/1 | | 18/7 | | 31/17 | | 19/9 | |
| Mexico City | F: | 66/42 | 4 | 77/51 | 14 | 73/53 | 27 | 70/50 | 13 |
| | C: | 19/6 | | 25/11 | | 23/12 | | 21/10 | |
| Moscow | F: | 21/9 | 11 | 47/31 | 9 | 76/55 | 12 | 46/34 | 11 |
| | C: | -6/-13 | | 8/-1 | | 24/13 | | 8/1 | |
| Paris | F: | 42/32 | 15 | 60/41 | 14 | 76/55 | 12 | 59/44 | 14 |
| | C: | 6/0 | | 16/5 | | 24/13 | | 15/7 | |
| Rio de Janeiro | F: | 84/73 | 13 | 80/69 | 10 | 75/63 | 7 | 77/66 | 13 |
| | C: | 29/23 | | 27/21 | | 24/17 | | 25/19 | |
| Rome | F: | 54/39 | 8 | 68/46 | 6 | 88/64 | 2 | 73/53 | 9 |
| | C: | 12/4 | | 20/8 | | 31/18 | | 23/12 | |
| Singapore | F: | 86/73 | 17 | 88/75 | 15 | 88/75 | 13 | 87/74 | 16 |
| | C: | 30/23 | | 31/24 | | 31/24 | | 31/23 | |
| Tokyo | F: | 47/29 | 5 | 63/46 | 10 | 83/70 | 10 | 69/55 | 11 |
| | C: | 8/-2 | | 17/8 | | 28/21 | | 21/13 | |

*Source: adapted from Hammond Travel Mate, Newsweek Inc.*

1. Which city has the highest average rainfall (for the four months given)?

_____

2. Which city is the dryest?

_____

3. Which city is the hottest?

_____

4. Which city is the coldest?

_____

5. Which city has the type of weather you prefer?

_____

## PLAN A TRIP

With a group of three students, consult the information from the tables above, and choose a city that you would like to visit. Describe to your class your choice of destination and the reasons your group chose it. Next, as a group, write a letter to its tourist board (addresses below), or visit a local travel agency to get more information. When you receive the information, read it, and create a poster advertising your destination. Include information from the tables in this chapter, as well as photos or information included in the promotional literature you received in the mail.

*IT WORKS!*
*Learning Strategy:*
*Cooperating*

Argentinean Tourist Information
330 West 58th Street
New York, NY 10019

Brazilian Consulate General
3810 Wilshire Blvd.
Los Angeles, CA 90010

British Tourist Authority
40 West 57th Street
New York, NY 10019

Egyptian Tourist Authority
323 Geary Street
San Francisco, CA 94102

French Government Tourist Office
610 Fifth Avenue
New York, NY 10020

Hong Kong Tourist Association
548 5th Avenue
New York, NY 10036

Italian Government Travel Office
630 Fifth Avenue
New York, NY 10111

Japan National Tourist Office
360 Post Street
San Francisco, CA 94108

Mexican Tourist Office
10100 Santa Monica Boulevard
Los Angeles, CA 90067

Russian Intourist
630 Fifth Avenue
New York, NY 10111

Singapore Tourist Board
342 Madison Avenue
New York, NY 10173

Spanish Tourist Office
665 Fifth Avenue
New York, NY 10022

Thailand Tourism Authority
3440 Wilshire Blvd.
Los Angeles, CA 90010

## PREREADING ACTIVITY

Freewrite for five minutes, using the name Christopher Columbus to start. Write whatever comes to mind, and do not worry about spelling or grammar!

## OBSERVATIONS AFTER LANDFALL

*Christopher Columbus[1]*

*friendship*

*that is, Catholicism*

I, in order that they might feel great amity° towards us, because I knew that they were a people to be delivered and converted to our holy faith° rather by love than by force, gave to some among them some red caps and some glass beads, which they hung around their necks, and many other things of little value. At this they were greatly pleased and became so entirely our friends that it was a wonder to see. Afterwards they came swimming to the ships' boats, where we were, and brought us parrots and cotton thread in balls, and spears and many other things, such as small glass beads and hawks' bells, which we gave to them. In fact, they took all and gave all, such as they had, with good will, but it seemed to me that they were a people very deficient in everything. They all go naked as their mothers bore them, and the women also, although I saw only one very young girl. And all those whom I did see were youths, so that I did not see one who was over thirty years of age; they were very well built, with very handsome bodies and very good faces. Their hair is coarse almost like the hairs of a horse's tail and short; they wear their hair down over their eyebrows, except for a few strands behind, which they wear long and never cut. Some of them are painted black, and they are the color of the people of the Canaries,° neither black nor white, and some of them are painted white and some red and some in any color that they find. Some of them paint their faces, some their whole bodies, some only the eyes, and some only the nose. They do not bear arms or know them, for I showed to them swords and they took them by the blade and cut themselves through ignorance. They have no iron. Their spears are certain reeds, without iron, and some of these have a fish tooth at the end, while others are pointed in various ways. They are all generally fairly tall, good looking and well proportioned. I saw some who bore marks of wounds on their bodies, and I made signs to them to ask how this came about, and they indicated to me that people came from other islands, which are near, and wished to capture them, and they defended themselves. And I believed and still believe that they come here from the mainland to take them for slaves. They should be good servants and of quick intelligence, since I see that they very soon say all that is said to them, and I believe that they would easily be made Christians, for it appeared to me that they had no creed. Our Lord willing, at the time of my departure I will bring back six of them to Your Highnesses,° that they may learn to talk. I saw no beast of any kind in this island, except parrots.

*Columbus is referring to people from the Canary Islands, off the coast of northwest Africa.*

*Columbus is writing to the King and Queen of Spain, Ferdinand and Isabella.*

[1]This passage was written hundreds of years ago. Therefore, it is written in a different style than something written recently would be. This may make it difficult to read at first, but try to focus on the meanings of the sentences. It may help to rephrase some of the more difficult ones.

Source: *The Journal of Christopher Columbus,* translated by Cecil Jane. Copyright 1960 by Clarkson N. Potter, Inc. In *Travels in the Americas,* J. Newcombe, Ed. (1989), New York: Grove Wiedenfeld, pp. 343-345.

## COMPREHENSION

Answer these questions without looking back at the reading.

1. Columbus gave the natives
   a. string and feathers;
   **b.** beads and hats;
   c. money;
   d. food and wine.
2. The natives wore
   a. reed clothing;
   b. feathers;
   **c.** nothing;
   d. leather suits.
3. The natives Columbus met were, according to his account,
   **a.** all young;
   b. of all ages;
   c. all male;
   d. all female.
4. Columbus believed that people from the mainland came to the island to
   a. trade goods;
   **b.** take slaves;
   c. declare war;
   d. collect parrots.

## ANALYSIS

The style of this reading may seem slightly strange, since it reflects a writing that is over 500 years old. Look at each of the sentences below, taken from the reading, and write them in a more modern style. Do not change the meaning of the sentences.

1. "At this they were greatly pleased and became so entirely our friends that it was a wonder to see."

   _____

   _____

2. "In fact, the took all and gave all, such as they had, with good will, but it seemed to me that they were a people very deficient in everything."

   _____

   _____

3. "They all go naked as their mothers bore them, and the women also, although I saw only one very young girl."

   _____

   _____

4. "They do not bear arms or know them, for I showed to them swords and they took them by the blade and cut themselves through ignorance."

_____

_____

_____

5. "They should be good servants and of quick intelligence, since I see that they very soon say all that is said to them, and I believe that they would easily be made Christians, for it appeared to me that they had no creed."

_____

_____

_____

_____

6. "I saw no beast of any kind in this island, except parrots."

_____

_____

## PREREADING QUESTION

Do you remember the first time you travelled on an airplane? Do you recall how you felt? Were you excited or frightened ? Discuss these questions with your class.

# EVENTS IN THE SKIES

## Doris Lessing

I once knew a man, a black man, who told me he had been brought up in a village so far from the nearest town he had to walk a day to reach it. Later he knew this "town" was itself a village, having in it a post office, a shop and a butcher. He had still to experience the white men's towns, which he had heard about. This was in the southern part of Africa. They were subsistence farmers, and grew maize, millet[1], pumpkins, chickens. They lived as people have done for thousands of years except for one thing. Every few days a little glittering aeroplane[2] appeared in the sky among the clouds and the circling hawks. He did not know what it was, where it came from or where it went. Remote, unreachable, a marvel, it appeared over the forest where the sun rose, and disappeared where it went down. He watched for it. He thought about it. His dreams filled with shining and fragile eminences that could sit on a branch and sign or that ran from his father and the other hunting men like a duiker[3] or a hare, but that always escaped their spears. He told me that when he remembered his childhood that aeroplane was in the sky. It connected not with what he was now, a sober modern man living in a large town, but with the tales and songs of his people, for it was not real, not something to be brought down to earth and touched.

When he was about nine his family went to live with relatives near a village that was larger than either the handful of huts in the bush or the "town" where they had sometimes bought a little sugar or tea or a piece of cloth. There the black people worked in a small gold mine. He learned that twice a week an aeroplane landed in the bush on a strip of cleared land, unloaded parcels, mail and sometimes a person, and then flew off. He was by now going to a mission school. He walked there with his elder brother and his younger sister every morning, leaving at six to get there at eight, then walked back in the afternoon. Later, when he measured distances not by the time it took to cover them, but by the miles, yards and feet he learned in school, he knew he walked eight miles to school and eight back.

This school was his gateway to the life of riches and plenty enjoyed by white people. This is how he saw it. Motor cars, bicycles, the goods in the shops, clothes—all these things would be his if he did well at school. School had to come first, but on Saturdays and Sundays and holidays he went stealthily to the edge of the airstrip, sometimes with his brother and sister, and crouched there waiting for the little plane. The first time he saw a man jump down out of its high uptilted front his heart stopped, then it thundered, and he raced shouting exuberantly into the bush. He had not before understood that this apparition of the skies, like a moth but made out of some substance unknown to him, had a person in it: a young white man, like the storemen or the foremen in the mines. In the village of his early childhood he had played with grasshoppers, pretending they were aeroplanes. Now he made little planes out of the silver paper that came in the packets of cigarettes that were too expensive for his people to smoke.

With these infant models in his hands the aeroplane seemed close to him, and he crept out of the bush to reach out and touch it, but the pilot saw him, shouted at him—and so he ran away. In his mind was a region of confusion, doubt and delight mixed, and this was the distance between himself and the plane. He never said to himself, "I could become a pilot when I grow up." On the practical level what he dreamed of was a bicycle, but they cost so much—five pounds—that his father, who had one, would need a year to get it paid off. (His father had become a storeman in a mine shop, and that job, and the move to this new place, was to enable his children to go to school and enter the new world.) No, what that aeroplane meant was wonder, a dazzlement of possibilities, but they were all unclear. When he saw that aeroplane on the landing strip or, later, that one or another in the skies, it made him dream of how he would get on his bicycle when he had one, and race along the paths of the bush so fat that. . .

When he had finished four years at school he could have left. He already had more schooling than most of the children of his country at that time. He could read a little, write a little and do sums rather well. With these skills he could get a job as a boss boy or perhaps working in a shop. But this is not what his father wanted. Because these children were clever, they had been invited to attend another mission school, and the fees meant the father had to work not only at the store job in the day time, but at night as a watchman. And they, the children, did odd jobs at weekends and through holidays, running errands, selling fruit at the back doors of white houses with their mother. They all worked and worked; and, again, walking to and from the new school took the children four hours of every day. (I once knew a man from Czechoslovakia who said he walked six miles to school and six miles back in snow or heat or rain, because he was a poor boy, one of eleven children, and this is what he had to do to get an education. He became a doctor.)

This man, the African, at last finished school. He had understood the nature of the cloudy region in his mind where the aeroplane still lived. He had seen much larger planes. He knew now the shining creature of his childhood was nothing compared to the monsters that went to the big airports in the cities. A war had come and gone, and he had read in the newspapers of great battles in Europe and the East, and he understood what aeroplanes could be used for. The war had not made much difference to him and his family. Then his country, which until then had been loosely ruled by Britain in a way that affected him personally very little (and he knew this was unlike some of the countries further south) became independent and had a black government. By now the family lived in the capital of the country. They had a two-roomed house in a township. This move, too, this bettering, was for the children. Now the brother took a job in a store as a clerk, and the sister was a nurse in the hospital, but he decided to go on learning. At last he became an accountant and understood the modern world and what had separated that poor black child he had been from the aeroplane. These days he might smile at his early imaginings, but he loved them. He still loved the little aeroplane. He said to himself: "It was never possible for me to fly an aeroplane, it never occurred to me, because black men did not become pilots. But my son. . ."

His son, brought up in a town where aeroplanes came and went every day, said, "Who wants to be a pilot? What a life!" He decided to be a lawyer, and that is what he is.

My friend, who told me all this, said, "My son would never understand, never in his life, what that little plane meant to me and the kids in the bush."

But I understood. On the farm where I grew up, once a week I watched a small aeroplane appear, coming from the direction of the city. It descended over the ridge into the bush on to the airstrip of the Mandora Mine, a Lonrho mine. I was transported with delight and longing. In those days ordinary people did not fly. A lucky child might get taken up for a "flip" around the sky, price five pounds. It was a lot of money, and I did not fly for years.

Last year I met a little Afghan girl, a refugee with her family in Pakistan. She had lived in a village that had water running through it from the mountains, and it had orchards and fields, and all her family and her relatives were there. Sometimes a plane crossed the sky from one of the larger cities of Afghanistan to another. She would run to the edge of the village to get nearer to that shining thing in the sky, and stand with her hands cradling her head as she stared up . . . up . . . up . . . Or she called to her mother, "An aeroplane, look!"

And then the Russians invaded, and one day the visiting aeroplane was a gunship. It thundered over her village, dropped its bombs and flew off. The house she had lived in all her days was rubble, and her mother and her little brother were dead. So were several of her relatives. And as she walked across the mountains with her father, her uncle, her aunt and her three surviving cousins, they were bombed by the helicopters and the planes, so that more people died. Now, living in exile in the refugee camp, when she thinks of the skies of her country she knows they are full of aircraft, day and night, and the little plane that flew over her village with the sunlight shining on its wing seems like something she once imagined, a childish dream.

[1] Maize and millet are types of grains used for food.

[2] "Aeroplane" is the British English form of "airplane."

[3] A small antelope from the southern part of Africa.

Source: *Granta* 22, Autumn 1987, pp. 14-17.

Doris Lessing is an important twentieth century British author who grew up in Rhodesia (now the countries of Zambia and Zimbabwe). Lessing often deals with African themes, as in her books *African Stories* and *The Grass is Singing*.

*IT WORKS!*
*Learning Strategy:*
*Asking for*
*Clarification*

## Threads

**The U.S. Forest Service** manages 175 national forest and grasslands on 191 million acres (77.29 million hectares).

## COMPREHENSION

Answer the following questions true or false without looking back at the reading.

_____ **1.** The African man of this story is uneducated.

_____ **2.** The author of this story is approximately the same age as her African friend.

_____ **3.** Black men did not become pilots when the African man was young.

_____ **4.** The African man's son is a pilot.

_____ **5.** The African man's family moved from a village to the city.

## ANALYSIS

Write six questions about this story which include the words listed below. Ask someone in your class each of your questions. Reword them if necessary, to help your partner understand. When you are asked a question, ask for help if you do not understand the question.

**1.** airplane, symbol

_____

**2.** son, pilot

_____

**3.** old man, education

_____

**4.** girl, Afghanistan

_____

**5.** old man, bicycle

_____

**6.** author, airplane

_____

## Themes

### DISCUSS

Review the discussion questions found in this chapter, either the ones you wrote, or ones that were already in this book. Choose one question you would like to discuss further. (If you can not find any, write a new one.) Ask your classmates your question.

---

---

### DEBATE

What type of vacation is best?

Some people climb mountains, bicycle across islands, or backpack across continents. Others'prefer to telephone for room service, and lie by the pool getting sun. Which is your preferred vacation—active or relaxing? In a group of four or more students, argue for your preferred vacation. Include as part of your argument the best place to take such a vacation.

Divide your group into two equal parts. Half of your group should argue for one side and the other side should argue for the other. Each side should get the same amount of time to present its arguments.

### ROLE-PLAY

> ### LEARNING STRATEGY
>
> **Overcoming Limitations: Using standard expressions and formulas makes you more fluent in idiomatic English and helps you overcome limitations.**

In this role-play, you should try to use as many "formulas" as seems natural. For example, "May I help you?" or "Thank you very much," are standard formulas used in many situations.

With a partner, imagine that one of you is a travel agent, the other a tourist wanting information about a trip she or he is planning. It may help to make a list of some standard phrases you might use in such a situation. Then role-play a scene in which the tourist visits the travel agent's office.

> ### Threads
>
> **Alaska Tourist Information:
> telephone
> 907-465-2010**

121

## WRITING

Think about the role that airplanes play in modern life. Reflect on the uses of airplanes in this chapter and in the chapter on war. What would life be like without airplanes? Write a description of how you think the world would be different if there were no airplanes. Try to include both positive and negative effects.

## The Cultural Dimension

*IT WORKS!
Learning Strategy:
Developing Cultural
Understanding*

1. Ask a classmate about his or her experiences with travel, specifically, what places has he or she visited in the world, and what were they like. Prepare at least five questions to ask about this topic. Report on your interview to the class.
2. Interview a U.S. resident about his or her experiences traveling to a foreign country. Prepare at least five questions about this topic. Tape record your interview or take detailed notes. Write a report on the results of your interview.

## Self-Evaluation Questionnaire

As you did in previous chapters, think about the goals you set at the beginning of the chapter. How well did you perform? Review your progress, then rate yourself in each of the following areas for this chapter. Give yourself the following ratings:

**5  excellent  4  good  3  average  2  fair  1  poor**

| | RATING |
|---|---|
| A.  Improved reading speed | ____ |
| B.  Understood main ideas | ____ |
| C.  Increased vocabulary understanding | ____ |
| D.  Learned more about the topic of the chapter | ____ |
| E.  Developed more understanding of style and grammar | ____ |

Compare your ratings with the objectives you set on the first page of this chapter.

# Space Exploration

## PLANNING & GOALS

List in order of priority (with 1 as 'most important') the objectives that are important to you in this chapter.

*IT WORKS!*
*Learning Strategy:*
*Setting Goals*

| GOAL | RANK |
|------|------|
| **A.** To increase reading speed | ____ |
| **B.** To increase comprehension of main ideas | ____ |
| **C.** To improve vocabulary understanding | ____ |
| **D.** To learn more about the information in this chapter | ____ |
| **E.** To improve understanding of style and grammar | ____ |

## LOOKING AHEAD

Space exploration is redefining what we think of as "travel." Just as the early explorers were pioneers in long-distance travel, astronauts are now expanding the usable territory of the universe. The idea of living in space is also becoming more of a reality. Furthermore, given the expense of such exploration, space travel is also offering new opportunities for global cooperation.

Look at the following titles of readings found in this chapter on space exploration.

"The Death of the Night," by E. Annie Proulx

"Star-swirls" a poem by Robinson Jeffers

"Manned Space Flight Controversy," letters

"Psst! Wanna Buy a Spaceship?" by James Oberg

*IT WORKS!*
*Learning Strategy:*
*Guessing*

Discuss the following questions with a partner.
1. Which of these titles interest you the most?
2. What do you know about space programs throughout the world today?
3. Would you like to travel into space? Why or why not?
4. Look ahead at the graphic material included in this chapter. What does it tell you about the subject matter?
5. What would you like to know about this topic? Write two or three questions you have about space exploration.

## Try a New Strategy

Language learning is not merely studying and classwork. It is important to have fun with the language in different ways. Try word games, crossword puzzles, and other language amusements.

## WORD SEARCH

Hidden in the grid below are words related to space exploration. They can occur forward, backwards, horizontally, vertically, or even diagonally. The hidden words are listed below the grid. As you find each word, cross it off the list. The first one is done for you.

| M | R | D | E | R | E | H | P | S | O | M | T | A | B | P |
| A | S | T | R | O | N | A | U | T | X | B | Q | S | I | L |
| R | P | O | X | N | O | T | Y | T | I | V | A | R | G | A |
| S | W | E | T | A | O | O | R | M | B | B | U | C | D | N |
| F | O | G | I | U | M | K | M | N | O | I | R | O | I | E |
| H | L | Y | J | Q | L | A | L | O | Y | N | A | O | P | T |
| S | G | R | U | R | P | P | T | X | U | V | N | J | P | S |
| E | R | U | A | Z | Z | O | A | S | Y | W | U | X | E | N |
| S | E | C | R | B | E | L | T | T | U | H | S | E | R | I |
| R | T | R | E | D | A | L | U | A | V | L | R | M | C | E |
| E | N | E | E | G | E | O | T | R | K | O | K | N | S | T |
| V | U | M | N | A | S | A | W | C | L | B | J | E | R | S |
| I | O | F | O | C | O | C | K | P | I | T | D | Q | K | N |
| N | C | Y | I | X | A | G | X | H | I | F | P | Y | O | I |
| U | Z | S | P | A | C | E | S | H | I | P | G | H | I | E |

**WORD LIST**

| | | | | |
|---|---|---|---|---|
| astronaut | Einstein | mercury | pioneer | Soyuz |
| atmosphere | explore | moon | planets | spaceship |
| Big Dipper | galaxy | NASA | Pluto | star |
| cockpit | gravity | orbit | shuttle | universe |
| counterglow | Mars | Orion | sky | Uranus |

## LISTENING

Locate videotapes of *The Right Stuff,* a film concerning the early U.S. space program, or some other space-related film. Check it out and watch it with a group of classmates. Answer the following questions and report to the class.

A.  Use the following spaces to take notes as you watch the film.
What was the name of the film you watched?

_____

What were the names of the main characters?

_____

_____

What were the most important events in the story?

_____

_____

_____

_____

_____

Describe your favorite scene.

_____

_____

_____

The title character from the 1982 film *E.T. The Extra-Terrestrial.*

### LEARNING STRATEGY

**Understanding and Using Emotions: Discussing your feelings can help you clarify your thoughts about what you read or listen to.**

B.  Discuss the following questions with your partners.
a.  Did you like this film? Why or why not?
b.  How did this film make you feel? (For example, happy, sad, etc.) Why?
c.  On a scale of 1–10, with 10 being the best, what rating would you give this film?

C.  As a group, compile your answers and give a report to your class about the film you watched. Include in the report the details of the movie, how well your group liked it, and what your reactions to the film were.

## PREREADING QUESTION

Do you enjoy "star-gazing," that is, looking at the stars, or trying to identify stars or planets? With a partner, compile a list of as many stars and planets as you can name. Compare your list to another pair's. How many did you name?

# THE DEATH OF THE NIGHT

*E. Annie Proulx*

I have the habit of looking up at hawks and clouds and stars. On clear nights I like to walk outside my house in central Vermont and be lifted into the vast wheel of the glittering sky. As a child I learned to search first for the Big Dipper and then, following its pointer stars, to find Polaris, the locus for skywatching in New England. The easiest constellation to detect was Orion and his tough dog, with its studded collar and pop eye. That eye is Sirius, a star that is 20 times brighter than the sun though far more distant.

At night I lie on the hillside to watch meteor showers. Sometimes I can see the northern lights, writhing streams of color in the upper atmosphere, agitated by solar winds. The look like a million miles of melting ribbon candy or the brilliant curving edge of tide on black sand.

A few months ago I drove north from Boston to Vermont. It was a clear night, and in an earlier year I could have seen the stars or an auroral display through a clean windshield. Not this time. All the way, until I was 20 miles from home, the sky was obscured by the orange smear of sodium vapor lights along streets and roads, emanating from parking lots, shopping malls, and fast-food parlors. When at last I turned onto the dirt road to home, I expected darkness. But here too the night was stained with light. It was at that moment I realized that this light was destroying the last remnants of natural darkness in rural New England.

Light pollution is endemic all over the earth, and astronomers in every observatory on the globe suffer from it. A few places near major observatories—San Diego County, Tucson, Phoenix, and Flagstaff—have enacted lighting ordinances.

Cities and suburbs have long since lost the sky, of course, but it's only been recently that the countryside has felt the effects. Rural electric utilities provide almost no help. In my part of Vermont, the Washington Electric Cooperative, whose rates are among the highest in the state, blithely promises its members substantial savings if they buy $45 kits to convert their mercury vapor lights to high pressure sodium lights. These lights are precisely the problem.

It takes a sort of visual patience to get to know the night. These days I'm remembering, rather than seeing, such phenomena as *gegenschein,* or counterglow. This is a delicate pale glow like a glass saucer in the dome of the sky around midnight, caused by reflected light from the sun, which, at that moment, stands exactly opposite, on the other side of the earth. The zodiacal light appears before dawn and after dusk, a cone of luminance emanating from the unseen sun below the horizon and disappearing into the zenith. Neither gegenschein nor zodiacal light can be seen in light-polluted skies.

Other fine distinctions are being obliterated. In the sprawl of the Milky Way all the stars, of staggeringly variable luminosities, look white at first, but as your eyes get used to the darkness the subtle colors show: red, blue-white, yellow, dull blue.

Our children are growing up blind to the sky, the first generation not to know its extraordinary beauty. It is a bitter loss.

Source: *New England Monthly, July 1990, pp 8-9.*

## COMPREHENSION

Answer these questions without looking back at the reading.

1. What is the main point of this reading?
   a. the joys of star-gazing
   b. astronomical phenomena in the Milky Way
   c. problems of light pollution
   d. electricity rates in the Northeast
2. What is another word for *gegenschein*?
   a. Polaris
   b. counterglow
   c. northern lights
   d. horizon
3. What does the author suggest as a solution to the problem?
   a. enact lighting ordinances
   b. install sodium vapor lights
   c. learn patience
   d. teach our children to enjoy the night sky

## ANALYSIS

1. Look at the map of the planets and their names. Do you know the corresponding names in your first language? Write them in the blanks. Are there any similarities?

Mercury  _____

Venus  _____

Earth  _____

Mars  _____

Jupiter  _____

Saturn  _____

Uranus  _____

Neptune  _____

Pluto  _____

2. Consult an encyclopedia or other reference book to find information about one of the following phenomena mentioned in this passage:
   a. Northern Lights (Aurora Borealis)
   b. *Gegenschein*
   c. Meteor showers
   d. Solar winds

Take notes from what you find and report to your class.

Edge of the Sun

Mercury

Venus

Earth

Mars

Jupiter

Saturn

Uranus

Neptune

Pluto

## VOCABULARY

The author of this article uses words to try to create images in the reader's mind. Look at the following descriptive sentences and paraphrase the italicized words or phrases in the following sentences from the reading.

1. On clear nights I like to walk outside my house in central Vermont and be lifted into the *vast wheel of the glittering sky.*

   _____

   _____

2. The easiest constellation to detect was Orion and his tough dog, with its *studded collar and pop eye.*

   _____

   _____

3. Sometimes I can see the northern lights, *writhing streams of color* in the upper atmosphere, *agitated* by solar winds.

   _____

   _____

4. The sky was obscured by the *orange smear* of sodium vapor lights along streets and roads, *emanating* from parking lots, shopping malls, and fast-food parlors.

   _____

   _____

5. Light pollution is *endemic* all over the earth, and astronomers in every observatory on the globe suffer from it.

   _____

   _____

6. This is a *delicate pale glow* like a glass saucer in *the dome of the sky* around midnight, caused by reflected light from the sun.

   _____

   _____

7. The zodiacal light appears before dawn and after dusk. *a cone of luminance emanating* from the unseen sun below the horizon and disappearing into the zenith.

   _____

   _____

8. In the *sprawl* of the Milky Way all the stars, of *staggeringly variable luminosities,* look white at first, but as your eyes get used to the darkness the subtle colors show.

   _____

   _____

### Threads

Light Year— (approx. 5,880,000,000,000 miles), distance light will travel in one year. Used in measuring distances in space.

IT WORKS!
Learning Strategy:
Visualization

## PREREADING ACTIVITY

As you read the following poem, try to picture in your mind the scenes the poet "paints" with words.

Star-Swirls

The polar ice-caps are melting, the mountain glaciers
Drip into rivers; all feed the ocean;
Tides ebb and flow, but every year a little bit higher.
They will drown New York, they will drown London.
And this place, where I have planted tree and built a stone house,
Will be under sea. The poor trees will perish,
And little fish will flicker in and out the window. I built it well,
Thick walls and Portland cement and gray granite,
The tower at least will hold against the sea's buffeting; it will become
Geological, fossil and permanent.
What a pleasure it is to mix one's mind with geological
Time, or with astronomical relax it.
There is nothing like astronomy to pull the stuff out of man.
His stupid dreams and red-rooster importance: let him count the star-swirls.

*Robinson Jeffers*

*Robinson Jeffers
(1887-1962)
was born in
Pittsburgh,
Pennsylvania. His
poetry focused on the
harsh beauty of nature.*

*The Beginning and the End and Other Poems*, 1963. New York: Random House, p. 18.

## ANALYSIS

1. Underline or highlight three lines or phrases that were easy to picture in your mind.
2. Underline or highlight any words you did not understand. Look them up in a dictionary and make notes of their meaning. Explain them to your partner.
3. In one sentence, summarize the main idea expressed in this poem.

## PREREADING QUESTION

The following reading consists of letters to a local Houston newspaper concerning the issue of sending people into space. Before you read this passage, take a poll of your class, asking everyone these questions.

a. Do you think space exploration is a worthwhile endeavor?
b. If there is limited funding, do you think money should go to programs on earth first?
c. Do you think space exploration benefits everyone? Why or why not?

# Manned Space Flight Controversy *

### Take care of domestic woes

As a high school student, I have grown up in an era of space flights and shuttle missions.

Like many others, I stand amazed at the feats of the National Aeronautics and Space Administration.

However, at the same time, I see the homeless, riots in Los Angeles and far too many problems within our own country.

Money should be shifted from defense and a mission to Mars and given to our own people.

With the $500 billion for a mission to Mars, we could provide homes for virtually every homeless and elderly person in our country.

Therefore, I don't feel the United States has to worry about competition, but it should be concerned about the domestic problems and needs of all its people, not space.

—Jennifer King, Huntsville, Texas

### It is just a waste of money

A manned space program is just a waste of money.

All of those billions and billions of dollars spent on the space program could do a great deal of good to the people here on this planet.

—Mrs. Jerusa G. Cantu, Houston, Texas

### We must strive to reach Mars

A manned space program is vital for mankind to learn more about its universe and the planets around us.

The goal of reaching Mars is as realistic as ever. We must strive for this goal to expand our knowledge.

The National Aeronautics and Space Administration's performance has been exceptional. It takes a lot to get a man up there and back. The years spent on each mission are endless.

There should be more funding and public support for current and future missions.

—Jason Bobruk, Huntsville, Texas

### Put space program on hold

It's time for our space program to be put on hold. Do away with the "cushy" jobs that NASA has become accustomed to enjoying.

At this point, the proposed $500 billion to put astronauts on Mars could be better spent putting Americas back to work.

—Loran E. Doss, Houston, Texas

### A successful path of discovery

Space Station Freedom is the next logical step for this country's manned space program. Are we going to shortchange future generations and not allow them to benefit as we have from the manned space program? Or are we going to continue on this successful path of discovery and give our children a chance to reach for the stars? How can we not afford the manned space program?

—Ann F. Sebesta, Pasadena

### Payback of program is positive

We Americans enjoy the fruits of the U.S. manned space program in our homes, schools, hospitals and businesses and we often take those benefits for granted.

NASA has done an outstanding job of providing an efficient, cost-effective and safe flow of technology from space via the space shuttle and will continue to develop those benefits through Space Station Freedom.

Every dollar spent on manned space programs was spent right here on Earth. Unlike many other programs, the payback has been very positive.

This program is one of the few that keeps the United States ahead in competitiveness.

—John F. Schuessler, Houston, Texas

### We need both technologies

No manned space program funds should be shifted. We need both a manned and unmanned program. The manned space station is at minimum configuration now. It should not be reduced. The unmanned program and expendable launch systems need more funding, however.

Robots and other devices can do some jobs . . . they could not have captured the satellite**. We need both technologies.

—Ralph E. Montijo, Houston, Texas

### Offering a future for the kids

I wholeheartedly support the efforts of NASA and its manned space program, which includes the space shuttle, Space Station Freedom and the mission to Mars.

I believe the cost of these problems is minute in comparison with the knowledge, technology and quality of life that is and can be derived from them. But I also believe that these programs offer perhaps intangible benefits that the United States cannot afford to lose: the future goals and dreams that it offers our children.

I do not know of any great, truly noble goal which our country has to offer our children besides this opportunity to explore the unknown and settle other lands. If we didn't have manned space programs, what future do we have to offer the young people of today?

—Ava Lunsford, Clear Lake City

*Houston Chronicle, May 23, 1992 (Section B, p. 3).*

* *Houston is the location of the National Aeronautics and Space Administration (NASA).*

** *The writer is referring to the capture of a communications satellite by three American space shuttle astronauts in May of 1992. The satellite had failed to go into proper orbit, and so the astronauts, during an unprecedented three-man space walk, caught the satellite so it could be relaunched.*

## ANALYSIS

1. The letters in the previous reading provide different points of view on the expenditure of money for a space program, in particular a space station. Review the letters and briefly note the arguments that the writers present, both for and against the space program.

### Threads

**Pioneer 3 was the first US spacecraft launched on December 6, 1958.**

| ARGUMENTS AGAINST THE SPACE PROGRAM | ARGUMENTS FOR THE SPACE PROGRAM |
|---|---|
| _____ | _____ |
| _____ | _____ |
| _____ | _____ |
| _____ | _____ |

2. Which side are you on? Do you think money spent on space research would be better spent elsewhere, or do you think it is money well spent? Add any additional arguments you can think of to the appropriate column.

3. Pair up with a classmate who holds a different position from yours. Explain who your opinion to your partner.

4. Write a "Letter to the Editor" like the ones you read above, explaining your opinion.

## ANALYSIS

Look at the advertisement and answer the following questions with a small group of classmates.

1. What product is being advertised?
2. What can you do with this product?
3. Would you be interested in purchasing this product? Why or why not?

## PREREADING ACTIVITY

Look at the table below. Examine the table with a partner, and describe the major events in the Soviet space program.

| DATE | NAME | CREW | ACCOMPLISHMENT |
|------|------|------|----------------|
| 4/12/61 | Vostok 1 USSR | Yuri Gagarin | First spaceflight by a human |
| 2/20/62 | Mercury 6 USA | John Glenn | First American orbital flight |
| 6/16/63 | Vostok 6 USSR | Valentina Tereshkova | First woman cosmonaut |
| 4/23/67 | Soyuz 1 USSR | Vladimir Komarov | First fatality of space program |
| 7/16/69 | Apollo 11 USA | N. Armstrong M. Collins E. Aldrin | First lunar landing |
| 6/6/71 | Soyuz 11 USSR | G. Dobrovolsky V. Patsayev V. Volkov | All 3 cosmonauts killed during re-entry |
| 5/25/73 | Skylab 2 USA | C. Conrad J. Kerwin P. Weitz | First Skylab launch |
| 4/12/81 | Columbia USA | J. Young R. Crippen | First use of a reusable space shuttle |
| 1/28/86 | Challenger USA | F. Scobee M. Smith R. McNair E. Onizuka J. Resnik G. Jarvis C. McAuliffe | Shuttle explodes on takeoff; all crew, including one civilian teacher, die. |
| 2/20/86 | Mir USSR | variable | Soviet space station launched |

The launching of the US space shuttle.

# PSST! WANNA BUY A SPACESHIP?

*James Oberg*

The voice on the telephone sounded hesitant and conspiratorial. "You don't know me," the caller disclosed unnecessarily, "but I need your advice." Fatalistically but patiently, I asked the man what it was all about. I get a lot of strange calls.

"What do you think we could sell a Soviet spaceship for?" he asked. "What kind of price might we expect?"

Not so long ago, I'd have immediately dismissed the offer as a crank call[1], but now that an economic crisis has hit the former Soviet Union, everything is for sale. The caller provided just enough obscure details about the hardware he was selling and the scientists he represented to earn credibility. Not long ago, the idea of swinging such a deal would have been a cosmic thrill, but such reactions had faded after the tenth or twentieth call.

As gently as I could, I informed my caller that entrepreneurs and even Soviet space officials in search of hard currency have flooded the market with Soviet space vehicles. The equipment he offered was the backup model to the two Fobos probes recently launched towards Mars and its small moonlets, an ambitious international project that promised to assay Martian resources and prove the feasibility of refining rocket fuel on site. Its success could have paved the way for the manned interplanetary flight within a decade or two. But both probes had failed miserably, and with the economic crisis precluding a second try, space officials tossed the backup hardware on the scrap heap to be sold for a few cents on the ruble.

The Fobos probe is a recent addition to an intriguing list that visiting Soviet scientists began handing out to Western space museums. It describes seventeen spacecraft and engineering mockups for sale but gives no prices.

Among the entries: a demonstration mockup of a Soyuz[2] landing craft "with three dummies, on stand"; a Soyuz-TM spacecraft demonstrated in France in 1988; a nose section of a Vertikal probe; a 1:5 scale model of the Buran shuttle; and, for the truly ambitious, a pair of full-scale Energiya super booster mockups—you pay for transportation.

Despite the Soviets' efforts, actual sales have been rare. A Sputnik[3] replica sold for $10,000, and a Japanese concern snapped up a Mir space station module for more than two million dollars then quickly resold it to a museum. By and large, potential customers have balked at the multi-million-dollar price tags on the other spacecraft. One Soviet group has demanded $1.6 million for a backup Venus probe and received not even a ruble.

"The Japanese ruined the market with that Mir deal," complains Fred Durant, the former top official of the Smithsonian's Air & Space Museum and now one of the world's leading authorities on spaceflight memorabilia and space art. "I'd have paid $150,000 to $200,000 for a flown Vostok," he says, but so far none have been sold. Much of the equipment for sale is somewhat unremarkable: "They have so *many* used reentry capsules."

Pricing the equipment has proved next to impossible because there is no sales history on which to base a price sale. Max Ary of the Kansas Cosmosphere had been offered training spacesuits for $10,000 by the manufacturers. "They don't know how to price it," he says, because, under the Communist system, they had no idea themselves how much the suits cost to make. In the course of his dealings with spacecraft purveyors, two groups often offered him the same hardware for prices that differed by as much as a few million dollars.

The spaceship sell-off has its limits, Durant observes. "It's not like these are the family jewels," he says, noting that nothing associated with first-in-space Yuri Gagarin[4] is for sale. "There's just so much of the stuff that they'll always have plenty left."

Other than the vast supply of space equipment, a primary stumbling block to significant sales remains lack of Western appreciation for Soviet space hardware. But that situation is being remedied even now by an unprecedented series of museum exhibits criss-crossing North America. Hundreds of thousands of Americans will now know the difference between a Progress and a Prognoz, a Soyuz and a Salyut, and a Mir and a Mriya.

With my survey nearly completed, my phone rang once more. "Jim, listen," began a journalist I knew from Washington, D.C. "I'm in touch with a Russian at the embassy who's working for a cosmonaut. They've got this Vostok rocket for sale, three million, negotiable. Where do you think we can find a customer?"

Oh no, I thought, not another one. But now at least their prices are negotiable. Maybe they're learning.

[1] A crank call is a joke, a non-serious phone call.

[2] Soviet space capsules (there were over 50 Soyuz flights made by the USSR). The first one was manned by Vladimir M. Komarov, and flew for nearly 27 hours. It made 18 orbits of earth, and cosmonaut Komarov was killed when the parachute failed. This was the first fatality of the space program.

[3] The Sputnik 1 was the first satellite to orbit earth, in 1957.

[4] On the Vostok 1, April 12, 1961.

Source: *Omni*, January 1992, p. 12.

### ANALYSIS

Discuss the following questions with a small group of classmates.

1. What was the man on the telephone trying to sell to the author of this article?
2. Why are the Soviets having difficulty selling their wares?
3. Why did Mr. Durant think the Japanese had "ruined the market with that Mir deal"?
4. With the political and economic instability in Eastern Europe, what do you think the future of the former Soviet space program will be?
5. Write another question you would like to add to this reading.

_____

_____

## SUMMARY EXERCISES

## Themes

### DISCUSS

Imagine that you have been selected to live on Mars in the new space colony. With a group of classmates, decide what "luxuries" you are going to bring along. You must discuss your choices and decide as a group.

a. Ten books: Which titles would you choose?
b. Fifteen cassette tapes or CDs: Which ones would you choose?
c. Five types of "junk food": Which ones?
d. Two paintings from any museum in the world (on loan, of course!): Which paintings or artists?

### DEBATE

Should people colonize space? What is your opinion?

Divide your group into two equal parts. Half of your group should argue for one side of the issue you chose, and the other side should argue for the other.

Use the following outline to help you develop your arguments.

State your side's opinion in one sentence:

_____

_____

_____

### Threads

Today we can no more predict what use mankind may make of the Moon than could Columbus have imagined the future of the continent he had discovered.

_Arthur C. Clark,
British author_

Reasons you believe this: (Again, state each reason as a sentence.)

1. _____

2. _____

3. _____

4. _____

(Use an additional piece of paper if you need more space.)

Present your debate to the class. Each side should get the same amount of time to present its arguments.

### ROLE-PLAY

Imagine that a committee is now interviewing people who will live in the space station. In a small group, two people should form the committee, and the rest should be potential space inhabitants. The committee should ask questions about a person's fitness and motivation for living in space. The applicants can be anyone you choose—an "invented" person, or you. Conduct the interviews and select the people who will be best suited for life in space.

### WRITE

Imagine that you are now living on the space station. What is life like? Write a letter home to Earth, explaining what your typical day is like.

## The Cultural Dimension

1. Interview a classmate about his or her country's involvement in space exploration. Prepare at least five questions to ask.
2. Interview someone outside of your class about his or her opinion of the future of the U.S. space program. Prepare at least five questions about this topic. Tape record your interview or take detailed notes. Write a report on the results of your interview.

At left: NASA astronauts repairing a satelite in space. Below: Photo from the joint Soviet/American space flight.

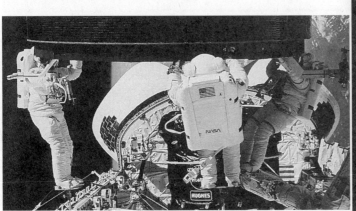

## Self-Evaluation Questionnaire

Make a list of new things you learned from this chapter.

1. _____
2. _____
3. _____
4. _____
5. _____
6. _____
7. _____
8. _____
9. _____
10. _____

As you did in previous chapters, think about the goals you set at the beginning of the chapter. How well did you perform? Review your progress, then rate yourself in each of the following areas for this chapter. Give yourself the following ratings:

**5 excellent  4 good  3 average  2 fair  1 poor**

| | RATING |
|---|---|
| **A.** Improved reading speed | _____ |
| **B.** Understood main ideas | _____ |
| **C.** Increased vocabulary understanding | _____ |
| **D.** Learned more about the topic of the chapter | _____ |
| **E.** Developed more understanding of style and grammar | _____ |

Compare your ratings with the objectives you set on the first page of this chapter.

# International Media

# PLANNING & GOALS

List in order of priority (with 1 as 'most important') the objectives that are important to you in this chapter.

*IT WORKS!*
*Learning Strategy:*
*Setting Goals*

| GOAL | RANK |
|---|---|
| **A.** To increase reading speed | _____ |
| **B.** To increase comprehension of main ideas | _____ |
| **C.** To improve vocabulary understanding | _____ |
| **D.** To learn more about the information in this chapter | _____ |
| **E.** To improve understanding of style and grammar | _____ |

# LOOKING AHEAD

As we have seen, travel and technology are improving our knowledge of the world. They are also improving our knowledge of the world through improved communication. Telecommunications, computers, and satellites all contribute to our ability to talk to nearly anyone, anywhere, anytime we wish.

The media is an important factor in this growing communications network. The news is no longer merely local, or national, but global. We can watch in our living rooms the problems of drought-stricken nations, or wars in other countries.

The following readings on communications technology and media and their influence make up this chapter.

"How Media Literacy Can Change the World," by Don Adams
    & Arlene Goldbard
"Compuserve," (advertisement)
"The Shrinking World of Totalitarian TV"
"Watch Local, See Global," by Danny Schechter

*IT WORKS!*
*Learning Strategy:*
*Guessing*

Before reading this chapter, discuss the following questions with a small group of classmates.

1. Which of the titles above interest you most?
2. Look ahead at the graphic material included in this chapter. What does it tell you about the subject matter?

3. What influence do you think television has on everyday life?

4. How has American or British television influenced the television programming shown in your own country?

5. What more would you like to know about this topic? Write two or three questions you have about international media.

## Try a New Strategy

Reviewing is an important part of learning. Take some time to look over the work you have done in earlier chapters. Reread the study questions and see how much you remember. Review regularly.

### LISTENING

As you did in Chapter 1, watch a national news show on ABC, CBS, NBC or CNN, then answer the questions in section A. In class, find a classmate who watched a different program, and complete the questions in part B.

Taking notes will help you to recall important details.

A. On your own, use the following spaces to take notes as you watch the news broadcast.

*IT WORKS!*
*Learning Strategy:*
*Taking Notes*

1. Name of television network you watched:

_____

2. Describe the major *international* news story of the day.

_____

_____

3. Was there any film shown as part of the story? If so, describe it.

_____

4. Describe one other international news stories that was reported on the program.

_____

_____

B. With a partner, complete the following‾

*IT WORKS!*
*Learning Strategy:*
*Asking for*
*Clarification*

1. Describe your answer for question 2 above to your partner. Try to recall all the details you can.

2. Describe your answer to question 4 to your partner. Explain which of the two stories you found most interesting, and why.

### PREREADING QUESTIONS

*IT WORKS!*
*Learning Strategy:*
*Highlighting*

Read the first sentence of the next reading. What do you think "critical thinking" is? Why might it be important to democracy? Highlight or underline important ideas in this reading.

STARTING TIME _____ : _____

# HOW MEDIA LITERACY CAN CHANGE THE WORLD

## *Don Adams & Arlene Goldbard*

Democracy requires critical thinking. Almost everyone agrees that the ability to read and write should be a fundamental human right, extended to everyone. We understand that a person who cannot read is in thrall to those who can. You cannot enter the developed world as a full human subject unless you can break and master the code of the word. Today, literacy doesn't stop with words and numbers. To enter social and political debates as a full participant one must also break the thrall of the magic box and master its secrets. If we fail to adopt media literacy—a basic knowledge of how and why media images are chosen—as an essential goal of public cultural policy, we doom ourselves to be forever in the grip of the powerful interests who own and control the mass media. The global proliferation of electronic mass media has excited deep feeling and passionate debate. Most alarming to observers around the world has been the passivity the mass media[1] seem to breed in most people; it displaces and undermines social life, community activities, and other creative pursuits. We jokingly call it being couch potatoes. As a society, we need to foster a more dynamic relationship between the citizenry and the media, one that does not stop when the program ends and the TV is turned off. For those who aspire to greater democracy in public life, our greatest challenge is transforming the media into a tool for democratic change.

Achieving this will require starting from square one. People without some special interest in the field find it hard to grapple with the idea that media is a public and political issue. This is not surprising since one of the things our mass media do best is pound home the inevitability of the way that they are currently organized, ideally suited to their role as the pep squad for our consumer society. Their self-ratifying quality makes it hard even to imagine that the media can be changed in any way.

The massive, interlocking complex of business interests that make up the mainstream media have been allowed to develop pretty much as they wish, in the pursuit of commercial success. Meanwhile, the essential public issue—the media role as our primary public forum, its tendency to erode democratic life—has been pushed further and further into the background.

It is necessary that we think about and promote a public policy that looks at what role media should play in our society and how people can participate in shaping television and other mass media that affect all of our lives. Such a public policy could counter the imbalances that result from the domination of a country's cultural industries by commercial interests. We cannot expect the commercial arena to accommodate the goals that should be the essence of this public policy: nurturing diversity, stimulating and supporting creativity, and encouraging active participation and interaction in community and political life.

[1] 'Media' is technically plural (the singular is medium), however, it is used both as singular and plural in modern usage. Therefore, you may see either "media is" or "media are" and both are correct.

Source: *The Independent Film & Video Monthly* August/ September 1989.

ENDING TIME _____ : _____
TOTAL TIME _____
491 WORDS ÷ _____ MIN = _____WORDS/MIN

## COMPREHENSION

How well did you understand this reading? Review your highlighting, and write a one or two-sentence summary of each paragraph.

_____

_____

_____

_____

_____

_____

_____

_____

_____

_____

_____

*IT WORKS!*
*Learning Strategy:*
*Summarizing*

Compare your summaries with another student's. Did you misunderstand, or miss, any of the author's important points? If so, you should rewrite your summaries.

## ANALYSIS

Look at the sentences below. Rephrase each sentence by substituting a synonym for the word or phrase that is italicized. You may have to change other parts of the sentence slightly, but do not change its meaning.

*IT WORKS!*
*Learning Strategy:*
*Vocabulary Focus*

1. We understand that a person who cannot read is *in thrall* to those who can.

_____

_____

2. To enter social and political debates as a full participant one must also break the *thrall* of the *magic box* and master its secrets.

_____

_____

3. We need to *foster* a more *dynamic* relationship between the *citizenry* and the media, one that does not stop when the program ends and the TV is turned off.

_____

_____

4. Achieving this will require starting from *square one.*

_____

_____

### Threads

**Average circulation for the Sunday New York Times: 1,762,015 newspapers**

**5.** This is not surprising since one of the things our mass media do best is *pound home* the inevitability of the way that they are currently organized, ideally suited to their role as the *pep squad* for our consumer society.

_____

_____

_____


**6.** The massive, *interlocking complex* business interests that make up the *mainstream media* have been allowed to develop *pretty much* as they wish, in the pursuit of commercial success.

_____

_____

## COMPREHENSION

Scan the advertisement and answer the following information:

**1.** What product is being advertised?

_____

**2.** What features does CompuServe offer?

_____

_____

**3.** How much does it cost to join CompuServe?

_____

_____

**4.** What do you think NYSE, AMEX, and OTC are?

_____

_____

## ANALYSIS

Ask a partner the following questions.

**1.** What CompuServe features interest you most?
**2.** Would you buy the CompuServe service?
**3.** If you can, find a computer store that can give you a demonstration of CompuServe or Prodigy, a comparable service. Report back to the class on what you learned. If you cannot locate such a store, call the 800 number given in the advertisement and receive more details by mail.

## PREREADING QUESTION

What is television programming like in other countries of the world? Discuss the types of television programs that are shown in countries with which you are familiar.

# THE SHRINKING WORLD OF TOTALITARIAN TV

### Broadcasting

Poland's top TV administrator last week provided a CNN-sponsored news conference a rare glimpse into the fast-disappearing world of totalitarian television.

Andrzej Drawicz, president, Polish Television, in a keynote address last Tuesday, Sept. 4, before a conference of CNN World Report contributors, told listeners that prior to the last few years' political change in Poland, "all information, and the news in particular, was not exactly to inform but rather to create a specific pseudo-reality. It was a peculiar anti-world, admittedly composed of actually existing elements [but] deformed by the intended indoctrination and thus false in the deepest sense."

The "uncanny world of Communist information," said Drawicz, was a "world of daily stress: which news to publish and which to conceal, which to distort completely and which in part only. . ." Such was the mythology of pseudo-information.

This official information's patent insidiousness, however, lent itself at times to mockery, Drawicz said, citing one satirist who "described the main news broadcast as propagating 'instructions how to cast steel, cap bottles and pack cottage cheese.'"

In another anecdote, Drawicz described how one evening in the spring of 1982, while the nation was still under martial law, the main news broadcast did not appear on air at its scheduled hour. "Minutes passed and guesses proliferated: coup d'état, journalists' revolt, sabotage, natural calamity?"

It was later learned that the broadcast, which finally began 20 minutes late, was delayed because the head of the Polish Army's main political headquarters and chief supervisor of television under martial law, decided the news announcer, a uniformed major, wore his

sideburns too long and so postponed the broadcast until he was tended to by a barber.

Despite government controls over media and information, Drawicz said that throughout Communist rule, many Poles regularly listened to foreign radio broadcasts in Polish aired by Radio Free Europe, Voice of America and the BBC.

"For many decades, the Poles learned from radio broadcasts what was really going on in their country and abroad," he explained. "A true war in the air started, its participants competing for the Polish listener's consciousness."

Under Poland's current government, the media have been provided far greater freedoms, the executive said. "We have become an important factor which contributes to the creation of Polish normalcy."

Drawicz warned, however, that caution is still required in dealing with government and party officials. "Leaders of the new parties watch us with distrust. They would like to be on TV as often and for as long as possible. Dissatisfied, they immediately accuse us of manipulations. Many of them would also like to make us their ally in a political game, while our motto necessarily has to be freedom from party adherence and impartiality."

Concluded Drawicz: "Our task is that of a competent and tactful intermediary between Poland and the rest of the world and vice versa. We are to educate the nation to live in a new Europe and a new world. . . Our intention is to contribute to the creation of freedom of information."

Following Drawicz's remarks, a number of media representatives from Eastern European countries discussed the impact of television on their revolutions and on the future of television in their countries.

Hungary was the first country to break from the communist past, and it was influenced by neighboring television from Austria, said Eugen Freund, correspondent for ORF, Austria's television network. Hungarians had access to ORF, who had their own correspondents in Eastern Europe. "Another influential factor was the appearance of dissidents from then Communist countries on Austrian television," said Freund. But the most significant event, he said, was the cutting of the barbed wire between the two countries of May 2, 1989, broadcast not only on ORF but on Hungary TV as well.

Freund said "TV has advanced the developments that were already on the move," giving people a feeling of togetherness. But television also raises their expectations of life and riches in the West, he said. Thousands of skilled workers are heading west, as borders open, he said, "in order to participate in what they perceive to be limitless wealth. . . The media is good enough to emotionalize, but it may lack the power for cool, candid analysis."

Elena Kudejova, a reporter for Bratislava in Czechoslovakia, discussed the difficulties in projecting objectivity in news reports. "The biggest problem is that a lot of our journalists are not used to criticizing or reacting to existing structures and systems," she said, because the government, in the past, dictated what the slant would be. Training in the west can be very useful, she said. But she said Czech reporters have a long way to go. A recent meeting between the Czech prime minister and a prime minister of a Czech republic went uncovered because the prime minister didn't want coverage because he didn't want any surprises.

Another problem she said is censorship, not from the government, but from journalists internally. "There are still people who wish us to prepare optimistic reports, not to bother viewers and not to disappoint them," she said.

Source: Broadcasting, September 10, 1991, p. 96.

## COMPREHENSION

Answer these questions without looking back at the reading passage. Fill in the blanks with the word that fits best (one word per blank).

Despite government controls over _____ and information, Drawicz said that throughout Communist rule, many Poles regularly listened to _____ radio broadcasts in Polish aired by Radio Free _____, Voice of _____ and the BBC.

"For many decades, the Poles learned from _____ broadcasts what was really going on in their _____ and _____," he explained. "A true war in the air started, its participants competing for the Polish listener's consciousness."

Under Poland's _____ government, the _____ have been provided far _____ freedoms, the executive said. "We have become an _____ factor which contributes to the _____ of Polish normalcy."

## ANALYSIS

Discuss the following questions with your class.

1. What do you think the government's role in the media should be? How much control should it have?
2. Do you think censorship ever serves a useful purpose? If so, under what circumstances? If not, why not?
3. How has television and radio influenced the recent revolutions in Eastern Europe?

## PREREADING ACTIVITY

Look at a recent copy of *TV Guide* or the newspaper television listings. How many international programs can you identify, including ones in languages other than English? Make a list of them, and share them with your class.

At home with satellite technology.

# WATCH LOCAL, SEE GLOBAL

*Danny Schechter*

In April, 1990, over half a billion people in 63 countries watched Nelson Mandela speak to a packed stadium of rock fans at a London concert in his honor. The only part of the world not watching was the biggest television market of them all—the United States.

Once again, American television was out of step with the world, isolationist and isolated in an increasingly globalized electronic community. Not one network here, including MTV or PBS[1], would touch what programmers apparently considered an event that was either too political or not adequately commercial or both. It was the American viewers who lost out this time—but in the long run it will be the folks who run our TV networks who will lose out if they bury their heads in the sands of outmoded thinking and status quo behavior.

American myopia[2] is not new, but strong economic pressures are now reshaping the nature of broadcasting and are likely to force the United States to jump on the emerging global television bandwagon.

Three powerful forces are at work:

First, the three major networks are facing a growing erosion of their viewing audience. Their power and popularity are shrinking, partly because of proliferating competition, partly because they are exhausted—when they are not insulting—as a creative and inspirational force.

Second, the spread of cable and satellite technology—and the penetration of VCRs—gives viewers more choice. The widespread use of remote controls has turned much TV viewing into expeditions in "zapping" as viewers dart through the dials looking for something compelling and usually find little of substance to engage their interest.

Third, production expenses are increasing even as viewership declines, forcing producers to seek less expensive programming methods. "Under the circumstances," writes Les Brown, one of our most respected writers about television, "there seems little choice for the U.S. networks but to deal abroad, cultivating the kinds of relationships with foreign suppliers they've had with Hollywood studios."

Already the big U.S. communications companies are buying up European production facilities and taking a stake in cable and newly privatized channels. (Japanese companies are also gobbling up U.S. firms.) As Europe approaches economic union in 1992, a vast new market is on the horizon. There are billions in pent up advertiser demand—with hundreds of hours of new programming needed. Americans want into this market, and Europeans—whose own TV program-making skills have matured significantly—want out. They are asking for access to the American market at the same time that U.S. companies seek to flood Europe with their product.

What this could mean is a new era in television—a chance for viewers everywhere to literally tune in the world and to be exposed to a diversity of voices, entertainment, and points of view. There's a danger, of course, that in this process cultures could be homogenized into one mushy TV soup by media moguls who see the world as The Deal of Fortune. But there is also the opportunity for television to realize Marshall McLuhan's[3] global village aspiration and become a force for the exchange of ideas, fashions, cultural events, and practical problem-solving across all borders and boundaries.

So far the American market has been resistant to diversity, for all of its talk of faith in free markets and fair trade reciprocity. U.S. programmers would much prefer to monopolize the terms of the international television interchange. American-made TV shows, from pro wrestling to religious pros like Jimmy Swaggart[4], are already shown worldwide. In contrast, foreign-made programming has a hard time penetrating our living rooms. Last year, only 7 percent of all prime time programming came from overseas—and that figure includes all the British imports on PBS.

This situation is not only unfair in the abstract; it deprives U.S. viewers of a window on the world. Our own parochialism is fed and reinforced by one-note news shows and march in lockstep with government and corporate agendas and by the freeze-out of entertainment, sports, and information from abroad. Our ability to relate to and emphatise with other

peoples will increase to the extent that we get a feel for their points of view, passions, heroes, humor, and cultural idiosyncrasies. An occasional overseas ambassador or president on "Nightline"[5] is not enough.

In this age of satellites, the technology exists to crack our cultural isolation and promote a cross-fertilization of ideas. Global programming is now technically feasible and economically viable. "World television" is poised to penetrate an insularity fed by the kind of educational underdevelopment that led to 60 percent of our high school kids not being able to find Japan on a globe and 20 percent not finding the United States.

Tuning in to the world need not be sold as something that's good for you, as some kind of elitist antidote to illiteracy. It can be marketed in the same way we market all TV shows—as worth watching, informative, or just plain fun. Already, broadcasters who are willing to take risks and introduce a more global perspective are getting a good viewer response. Ted Turner[6] has built CNN on the strength of its overseas reach, and he is now making money as a global broadcaster. The Discovery Channel[7] is also doing well with programming with international themes.

The success of Globalvision's weekly television newsmagazine "South Africa Now" illustrates the potential for innovative global programming. Hailed by *Time* magazine for filling a void in news coverage, the show recently won an Emmy award for its coverage, supplied mostly by black South African video teams. "South Africa Now" is seen on 80 PBS stations and also in the Caribbean, southern Africa, Canada, and Japan. It contributes stories weekly to CNN's "World Report".

Globalvision is now developing several other programs on the "South Africa Now" model, fusing cultural and news segments. They include "The Soviet Union Now", produced jointly by Russians and Americans, and "Rights and Wrongs", a global human rights show. In the commercial sphere, an international magazine show offering to bring "the best of the world to the rest of the world" is in the final stages of pre-production with a number of international broadcasters and production groups already expressing strong interest. This show will aim to bring a mix of international television into the U.S. TV market in a package attractive for U.S. viewers. It will also provide customized editions for viewers in other countries, in their own language.

Companies like Globalvision can't single-handedly change the dismal state of TV programming, but they are determined not to leave it the same either. As we approach the turn of the century, as TV thrusts itself on the cutting edge of change from Romania to South Africa to Tiananmen Square, it is no longer a question of *whether* we will see what the world sees, but when. Soon we'll be watching local—seeing global!

[1] MTV is Music TV, a cable television station, and PBS refers to the Public Broadcasting System, a noncommercial television network.

[2] Shortsightedness.

[3] A writer famous for his books on the popular media and communication.

[4] A Christian minister with a popular television. show

[5] A popular late-night news talk program, seen on ABC.

[6] Media mogul who owns several television stations seen on cable, including CNN (Cable News Network). He is currently married to the actress Jane Fonda. – now divorced

[7] A cable television station dedicated to showing documentaries, nature shows, and news programs.

Source: *Z Magazine,* April 1988, as reprinted in *Utne Reader* 40 July/August 1990, pp. 76–79.

ENDING TIME _____ : _____
TOTAL TIME _____
1144 WORDS ÷ _____ MIN = _____WORDS/MIN

## COMPREHENSION

Answer the following questions true or false without looking back at the reading passage.

_____ 1. The 1990 Nelson Mandela speech in London was seen by 63 countries, including the U.S.

_____ 2. Economic pressure is reshaping American television.

_____ 3. American television networks are more popular than ever.

_____ 4. Television viewers have more choices because of VCRs and cable.

_____ 5. U.S. communications companies are buying private TV channels in Japan.

_____ 6. The U.S. receives only 7 percent of its prime time programming from foreign countries.

## ANALYSIS

Answer the following questions and share them with a partner, preferably one from a culture different from your own.

1. Is there any national television program from your own country that you wish were on in the U.S.? Describe a program shown in your country that you think could be popular in the U.S.
2. What U.S. television programs are shown in your country?
3. What sort of international programming would you like to see, both in the U.S. and abroad?

## VOCABULARY

Several places in this reading contain *clichés,* idiomatic phrases that are used frequently to get a particular idea across. Find the following clichés in the reading, and see if you understand their meanings. Then use them again in a sentence of your own creation.

*IT WORKS!*
*Learning Strategy:*
*Recognizing*
*Formulas*

1. bury their heads in the sand

_____

_____

2. jump on the bandwagon

_____

_____

3. a window on the world

_____

_____

Drawing by Modell; © 1989
*The New Yorker* Magazine, Inc.

*"What'll it be—entertainment news or entertainment?"*

## ANALYSIS

What does the man in the cartoon mean by "entertainment news"?

# SUMMARY EXERCISES

## Themes

### DISCUSS

*IT WORKS!*
*Learning Strategy:*
*Note Taking*

What is censorship? Compare the articles about television in Poland and in the U.S. Is censorship a factor in both systems? How is censorship different in these two countries? Discuss these questions, and any others you might think of concerning censorship, with your class. Make notes of the major points made during the discussion.

### DEBATE

With a group of classmates, review your notes from the class discussion and develop a topic for debate. Divide your group into two equal parts. Half of your group should argue for one side of the issue you chose, and the other side should argue for the other.

You may want to use the following outline to help you develop your arguments.

Topic:

_____

State your side's opinion in one sentence:

_____

_____

What are the reasons you believe this? (Again, state each reason as a sentence).

1. _____
2. _____
3. _____
4. _____

(Use an additional piece of paper if you need more space.)

Present your debate to the class. Each side should get the same amount of time to present its arguments.

## ROLE-PLAY & WRITE

Create your own news broadcast. With a small group of classmates, find a current newspaper and read the major stories. From these stories, create a television news script; that is, turn each major story into a one- or two-minute broadcast script. Practice reading your scripts, and then give your news broadcast for your class.

## The Cultural Dimension

1. Where do you get most of your information about the world? Take a poll of your classmates, or any other group of ten or more people, and ask them this question, along with three more questions about television and its influence.
2. Interview someone outside of your class about his or her opinion of the media and the work it does. Prepare at least five questions about this topic. Tape record your interview or take detailed notes. Write a report on the results of your interview.

*IT WORKS!
Learning Strategy:
Developing Cultural
Awareness*

## Self-Evaluation Questionnaire

Make a list of new things you learned from this chapter.

1. _____
2. _____
3. _____
4. _____
5. _____
6. _____
7. _____
8. _____
9. _____
10. _____

As you did in previous chapters, think about the goals you set at the beginning of the chapter. How well did you perform? Review your progress, then rate yourself on how you did in each of the following areas for this chapter. Give yourself the following ratings:

**5 excellent  4 good  3 average  2 fair  1 poor**

| | RATING |
|---|---|
| **A.** Improved reading speed | _____ |
| **B.** Understood main ideas | _____ |
| **C.** Increased vocabulary understanding | _____ |
| **D.** Learned more about the topic | _____ |
| **E.** Developed more understanding of style and grammar | _____ |

Compare your ratings with the objectives you set on the first page of this chapter.

# Religion

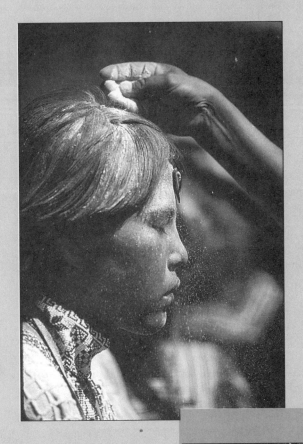

## 9
### CHAPTER

## PLANNING & GOALS

*IT WORKS!*
*Learning Strategy:*
*Setting Goals*

List in order of priority (with 1 as 'most important') the objectives that are important to you in this chapter.

| GOAL | RANK |
|------|------|
| **A.** To increase reading speed | ____ |
| **B.** To increase comprehension of main ideas | ____ |
| **C.** To improve vocabulary understanding | ____ |
| **D.** To learn more about the information in this chapter | ____ |
| **E.** To improve understanding of style and grammar | ____ |

## LOOKING AHEAD

Religion plays a major role in the world's cultures—not merely at personal and spiritual levels, but in the organization of societies. Religion can be the road to harmony, or to major conflict. Understanding a group's religion can help you understand its values and concerns.

This chapter deals with the subject of religion throughout the world. The following readings make up the chapter.

"Ohiyesa"

"Early Islam" by N. Minai

"Pashu Lama: Meditation and Manacles," by Nick Gregory and Thomas Laird

"Craigavon Bridge," by Seamus Deane

1. Which of the titles above intrigue you the most?
2. Look ahead at the graphic material included in this chapter. What does it tell you about the subject matter?
3. Review the reading "The Global Village," in Chapter 2 (p. 34). What are the major religions of the world?

### Try a New Strategy

What is your ideal environment for reading? Think about where and when you like to read. Do you prefer silence, or do you like to listen to music? Write a description of the best conditions for reading, then try to create those conditions as often as possible.

156

## LISTENING

Many movies have treated the issue of religion and its influence. Go to a local video store, or using a video guide, locate three films that have dealt with religion as a major theme:

The names of the films you found:

1. _____

2. _____

3. _____

With a partner or small group, check out and watch one or more of these films, and report on it to your class. Use the following questions to guide your report.

**1.** The name of the movie you watched:

_____

**2.** What were the names of the main actors in the film, and what were the names of the characters they played?

ACTOR                                    CHARACTER

_____        _____

_____        _____

_____        _____

_____        _____

_____        _____

**3.** Which religion or religious issue was treated in the film?

_____

**4.** Describe the story of the film, briefly.

_____

_____

**5.** Describe a memorable scene from the film. Try to recall all the details you can.

_____

_____

_____

**6.** Did you like the movie? Why or why not? _____

_____

_____

_____

### Threads

**Over 1,016,400,000 people in the world have no religion.**

Universal Almanac 1992
(Andrews and McMeel)

7. Would you recommend that others see this film?

_____

8. On a scale of one to ten (with ten being best), what rating would you give this film? _____

As a group, present a report to your class on the film you chose.

## PREREADING QUESTION

What do you know about Native American Indians? How do you imagine their life to be before the coming of the Europeans? Discuss these questions with your class before reading the next passage.

*IT WORKS!*
*Learning Strategy:*
*Use Your Knowledge*

### OHIYESA[1]

In the life of the Indian there was only one inevitable duty,—the duty of prayer—the daily recognition of the Unseen and Eternal. His daily devotions were more necessary to him than daily food. He wakes at daybreak, puts on his moccasins° and steps down to the water's edge. Here he throws handfuls of clear, cold water into his face, or plunges in bodily. After a bath, he stands erect before the advancing dawn, facing the sun as it dances upon the horizon, and offers his unspoken orison°. His mate may precede or follow him in his devotions, but never accompanies him. Each soul must meet the morning sun, the new sweet earth and the Great Silence alone!

Whenever, in the course of the daily hunt the red hunter comes upon a scene that is strikingly beautiful or sublime—a black thundercloud with the rainbow's glowing arch above the mountain, a white waterfall in the heart of a green gorge°; a cast prairie tinged with the blood-red of sunset—he pauses for an instant in the attitude of worship. He sees no need for setting apart one day in seven as a holy day, since to him all days are God's.

*type of leather shoe*

*prayer*

*canyon or large "gulch"*

[1]Ohiyesa, a Santee Dakota Native American, was a physician and writer. This piece was written in 1911.

Source: *Touch the Earth,* 1971 T.C. McLuhan, (ed.) New York: Simon & Schuster, p. 36.

## COMPREHENSION

Answer these questions without looking back at the reading. Fill in the blanks with the appropriate word (one word per blank).

1. In the life of the Indian there was only one inevitable duty,—the duty of _____.

2. He wakes at daybreak, puts on his _____ and steps down to the water's edge.

3. After the _____, he stands before the dawn, facing the sun as it dances upon the _____, and offers his unspoken _____.

4. Each soul must meet the morning _____, the new sweet earth and the Great Silence _____!

5. Whenever, in the course of the daily hunt the red hunter comes upon a scene that is _____, he pauses for an instant in the attitude of _____.

6. He sees no need for setting apart one day in _____ as a _____ day, since to him all days are God's.

## ANALYSIS

"The Global Village," in Chapter 2 mentions the religion "Animist." What is animism? With a small group, look up animism in an encyclopedia or other reference work. Take notes on what you find. Discuss the following questions with your group.

1. Think about the description of animism and Ohiyesa's writing. Do you see evidence of animist beliefs in this writing?
2. What comparison is Ohiyesa making in the last sentence of this reading?
3. (Write another question to add to this reading.) _____

_____

_____

### LEARNING STRATEGY

**Remembering New Material: Associating facts or words by using acronyms (initials) or other memory strategies can help you remember them better.**

The traditional blessing given during a Jewish wedding ceremony.

## PREREADING ACTIVITY

The following table will help you understand the reading that follows it. Highlight a key word for each entry to help you remember the events listed. Then, using the *first initial* of each of the key words, create a meaningful sentence (this can even be in your first language) to recall the important words.

For example, for the first three entries you might highlight the names "Muhammad, Abu Bekr, and Fatima." You could remember these three names by creating the phrase: "*Many apples, berries, figs*" (M=Muhammad, A=Abu B=Bekr, F=Fatima).

### A BRIEF HISTORY OF EARLY ISLAM

| YEAR | EVENT |
|---|---|
| 570 | Mohammad, founder of Islam, is born |
| 573 | Abu Bekr, Mohammad's father-in-law and first Caliph of the Mohammadans is born |
| 606 | Fatima, daughter of Mohammad, is born |
| 610 | Mohammad has a vision on Mount Hiraa |
| 615 | The earliest records of some of Mohammad's teachings |
| 622 | The Hegira—Mohammad flees from Mecca to Medina—Year One in the Moslem calendar |
| 624 | Mohammad marries Khadija, the daughter of Abu Bekr |
| 625 | Mohammad begins to dictate the Quran |
| 627 | Mohammad's enemies from Mecca take siege of Mecca and kill 700 Jews |
| 628 | Mohammad takes Mecca and writes letters to the world's rulers, explaining the Moslem faith |
| 632 | Fatima, Mohammad's first daughter and mother of Hassan and Hussein, founder of the House of Fatimids, dies. Mohammad also dies this year. |
| 650 | Caliph Othman puts the Quran into 114 chapters |

Source: adapted from *The Timetables of History,* by Bernard Grun, New York: Simon & Schuster, 1982.

# EARLY ISLAM

## Naila Minai

While mediating alone one day in the cave, Muhammad heard a voice which he believed to be the angel Gabriel's. "Proclaim in the name of thy Lord and cherisher who created, created man out of a clot of congealed blood" (*Quran,* surah [chapter] 96, verses 1-2), it said, pointing out that there was only one God and that man must serve Him alone. When Muhammad recovered from his ecstasy, he ran back, shaken, and described his experience to his wife. Having shared his spiritual struggles, Khadija understood that her husband had received a call to serve the one God whom the Christians and the Jews also worshiped. Bewildered and confused, Muhammad went on with his daily work in the city and occasional meditations on Mount Hiraa. Again the voice commanded him to tell his people about the one omnipotent God, who would welcome believers into heaven and cast wicked people into hell. With Khadija's repeated encouragement, Muhammad finally accepted his prophetic call and devoted the rest of his life to preaching God's word as the new religion of Islam (which means *submission* [*to the will of God*]). Converts to it were called Muslims (*those who submit*). They were not to be called Muhammadans, because they did not worship Muhammad, who was merely a human messenger for the one God. Though invisible and immortal, this God was named Allah after the Zeus of the old Meccan pantheon.

Numerous revelations that Muhammad received from Allah throughout his life were compiled shortly after his death into the Muslim bible, named the Quran, which formed the basis for the Shariah, or Islamic law. A supplement to it was provided by the Hadith, or Muhammad's words, which were recorded over many years as his survivors and their descendants remembered them. Despite the exotic Arabic words in which it is couched, Islam's message is similar in its essentials to the one promulgated by Judaism and Christianity, and can be summed up by the Ten Commandments. *Allah,* after all, is but the Arabic name for the God worshiped by both Jews and Christians. But the rituals differed. Muhammad required his followers to obey the commandments through the practice of five specific rituals, called the pillars of Islam. A Muslim must (1) profess faith in one God; (2) pray to him; (3) give alms to the poor; (4) fast during Ramadan, the month in the lunar calendar during which Muhammad received his first revelation; and (5) go on a pilgrimage to Mecca at least once in his lifetime (if he can afford to do so) to pay respects to the birthplace of Islam and reinforce the spirit of fellowship with Muslims from all over the world.

From *Women in Islam,* New York: Seaview Books, 1981.

## COMPREHENSION

Answer these questions without looking back at the reading passage. Write the letter of the correct answer in the blank by each question.

a. Shariah     b. Mt. Hiraa     c. Allah     d. Hadith
e. Khadija     f. Ramadan     g. Mecca     h. Quran

_____ 1. Where did Muhammad meditate?

_____ 2. What is the name of the Muslim holy book?

_____ 3. What was Muhammad's wife's name?

_____ 4. What is the Arabic name for God?

_____ 5. What is the name for Islamic law?

_____ 6. What is the name for Muhammad's words, which were recorded by his survivors?

_____ 7. What is the name of the fasting period?

_____ 8. To what place is there an annual pilgrimage?

## ANALYSIS

Refer to the reading, and create a list of the major beliefs of Islam. How are these beliefs similar to or different than any other religion with which you are knowledgeable?

| | ISLAM | OTHER |
|---|---|---|
| 1. | _____ | _____ |
| 2. | _____ | _____ |
| 3. | _____ | _____ |
| 4. | _____ | _____ |
| 5. | _____ | _____ |
| 6. | _____ | _____ |
| 7. | _____ | _____ |
| 8. | _____ | _____ |
| 9. | _____ | _____ |
| 10. | _____ | _____ |

## PREREADING ACTIVITY

Look at the photograph of the Pashu Lama. Freewrite for five minutes about this photograph. Use the following questions to get you started, if necessary:

- What sort of person do you imagine the Pashu Lama to be?
- What emotion does the photo cause for you? Joy? Pleasure? Something else?

As in other freewriting assignments, do not be concerned with spelling or grammar. Just write whatever comes to your mind.

The Pashu Lama in 1990.

# PASHU LAMA:
# A MEDITATION AND MANACLES

## Nick Gregory & Thomas Laird

He appeared from a dark doorway in the Nachung Monastery in Lhasa: a rotund smiling old man in tattered grey robes, his hands overflowing with walnuts. He couldn't hold on to all the walnuts he was offering me. They clattered on the ground as his dog ran around him barking. He was hushing the dog, laughing at having too many walnuts, giving them to me and inviting me into his room all at once. His infectious smile and laughter were impossible to resist. In the room there would be endless cups of tea thick with rancid yak butter. Is butter tea too high a price to pay for enlightenment? I followed him and then the first cup was in my hand and as he offered it I saw the scars. They were deep scars, the marks of manacles clamped tight for many years.

His name was Pashu Lama and he was a spiritual leader of one of the world's oldest faiths.

In case you were in any doubt, rest assured that the old adage[1] is true: religion thrives under persecution. A century ago, Tibetan Buddhism appeared to Westerners as a strange ritual practiced in a lost country behind the Himalayas. Then in 1959 the Chinese invaded Tibet and the persecutions began. Monks and nuns were forced to marry and to destroy the monasteries in which they had spent their lives. Abortive rebellions arose, to be quickly crushed by a Chinese leadership in the throes of the Cultural Revolution. As conditions deteriorated, Tibetan refugees began to move out, first into Asia, then to the West. They took their beliefs with them, and so the ideas of Tibetan Buddhism became increasingly familiar to the outside world.

The persecutions have continued now for 30 years, and with each passing year the religion of compassion and nonviolence that the persecutors have tried to suppress has grown stronger. You could spend a lifetime trying to understand Buddhist beliefs. Or you might understand them in one intuitive flash—then spend a lifetime trying to practice your understanding.

At their heart are a few deceptively simple ideas. One is to renounce all attachment to the world—"A dream, a flash of lightning and a cloud; Thus we should look upon the world" (*Vajracchedika sutra*). Yet at the same time one must give oneself to the world with unqualified compassion for all living things.

Such compassion inevitably implies nonviolence. When Mahatma Gandhi[2] chose to transform the politics of India by nonviolent means he was a man ahead of his times. Today the idea of peaceful change has its own compelling logic in a far more dangerous world than Ghandi knew. A leading exponent of this doctrine of nonviolence is the Dalai Lama, a spiritual leader of the Tibetan Buddhists. In 1989, he received the Nobel Peace Prize in recognition that the beliefs of his faith are of fundamental importance to our world.

The Pashu Lama, like his leader the Dalai Lama, understands these beliefs; his entire life is an expression of that understanding. The beliefs and the man who holds them have become indistinguishable.

The Tibetans believe we live through many lifetimes. In each lifetime we acquire merit—or its reverse—according to our actions. Great teachers (lamas) are those who have acquired great merit in their former lives. Pashu Lama is one of those; a great teacher in patched and tattered robes, sipping tea in a small bare room.

I ask him about his past lives—his previous incarnations[3]. But I am thinking of his bare surroundings and simple clothing, and when he speaks it is these thoughts that he answers.

"We don't care about money and fine clothes or other outer things. They aren't important. We must meditate—simply meditate. We should watch what our eyes are looking at. We should watch what our mind is thinking. We should watch what our ears are hearing."

He laughs again and offers me more butter tea.

Pashu Lama began to study the Buddhist path in 1913, when he was six years old. He followed the rigorous training of a monk for 20 years—rising before dawn for long hours of meditation. Studying traditional texts, learning to debate and interpret obscure points of Buddhist teaching. And slowly making the inward pilgrimage to what the Buddhists call enlightenment.

"I had completed the 20-year course when I began to say some crazy things." He gives me a huge grin. "At the monastery people said I was talking too much. They'd say 'That guy is mad.'"

This was when the monks realized that Pashu Lama was the reincarnation of one of the great lamas of the past. He was made the Khenpo, or head, of the monastery where he had first studied as a child.

"Later I was called to Kunda Ling monastery. They had heard of my madness so when their

lama died I was asked to help out until he was reborn."

"So what were you doing?" I ask. "What happened in all those years before the Chinese arrived?"

He lifts himself erect and for a moment is the embodiment of immense pride. Then his burst of laughter punctures the illusion and he is himself again. "I was just sitting around meditating."

Without a sign of rancor he points to the manacle scars on his wrists. "Then the Chinese came and I went to jail for seven years."

He was 56 years old when the Chinese invaded Tibet. Until then the country had been ruled by the lamas, and the Chinese were determined to break what they saw as the power of religious superstition over the Tibetan people. And so began a 30-year process of trying to separate the Tibetans from their religion. Many of the high lamas were imprisoned, including the Pashu Lama, who was one of those the Chinese saw as leading members of the "exploiting class."

After seven years a faint breath of freedom stirred in China. Tibet was named an Autonomous Region and many prisoners, including Pashu Lama, were released. In Beijing, Mao watched the changes for a time, then reversed them in that explosion of national self-destruction known as the Cultural Revolution[4]. The hesitant moves toward liberalization in Tibet ended. And once more the prisons opened.

"All I did was meditate for the two years I was out of jail, so they put me back in for another eleven years. I was in various camps in China and Tibet. I shoveled shit and broke rocks. Sometimes I could meditate. Sometimes things were such that I couldn't. I was able at least to keep my mind on His Holiness the Dalai Lama."

All this is said in a lighthearted tone, but when he mentions the Dalai Lama his eyes roll inward, leaving only the whites exposed, and for a moment I have the sense that everything is posed in stillness. Then he brings his palms together in front of his heart in the universal sign of devotion and breaks out again into smiles.

"The Chinese said 'You are a high lama and you cheated the people.' Then they would beat me and chain me up."

With raised finger and aloof expression he momentarily imitates to perfection a petty bureaucrat; the next moment he is a furious jailer, invisible stick in hand, about to beat this idiot of a prisoner. He switches from one personality to another instantaneously. Then he is himself again. I have the sense that he doesn't see the distinctions between people in the same way that I do.

"You know what Karma is?"

I nod. Karma—as I understand it—is the way in which the consequences of our actions, perhaps from a previous life, affect us in the future.

"I thought 'Maybe I had a little bad Karma I have to pay for.'" Then he adds, "The Chinese had special punishments for me because of what I am. But I recalled that the Buddha is not dead and I meditate on the Dalai Lama."

I think of the special punishments, but ask instead how he had been able to deal with such a great change in his life—from High Lama to ill-treated prisoner. "Who had time to think about the past? My mother was dying in jail at the age of 76. My father was dead. All I could concentrate on was the Buddha and the Dalai Lama.

"These days I have good hope that through the grace of his holiness the Dalai Lama and with the watchfulness of all our Western friends, the days of religious persecution are over once and for all. I hope that slowly now Tibet will be opened and we will be given more friends.

"We have had some Karma to go through, as a people and as far as I myself am concerned. That's why we have experienced these things. Our future freedom—that of Tibet and my own—is up to our Karma."

Of more than 6,000 monasteries in Tibet before the invasion, only a handful are left standing. From the stories that refugees bring out of Tibet it appears that an entire culture is being systematically eradicated. Tibetans still flee their country and many tell all-to-convincing stories of torture. But for Pashu Lama these things are Karma—he sees the workings of the laws that delineate the Buddhist world, and he blames no one.

It has been impossible for me to return to Tibet and I have had no news of Pashu Lama. Perhaps—probably—he is dead. He would regard death as merely a transition state between the countless lives that lie between now and enlightenment.

When I left him he said:

"I would be happy if you would publish my story with my real name. There are no lies in what I have said. I have no living relatives. I'm 80 now. I would be proud for others to hear this story.

"If you tell the truth it will never die and in its result will be truth again."[5]

[1] Motto, slogan, or saying.

[2] Mahatma Gandhi, 1869-1948 was the leader of Indian nationalism. He was dedicated to the ideals of non-violence.

[3] One important aspect of Buddhism is the belief in prior lives, or incarnations.

[4] The Cultural Revolution ocurred in China during the 1960s. It was a time when many people were imprisoned if it was believed that they were not faithful to the principles of communism.

[5] Pashu Lama died peacefully in the fall of 1990.

Source: *Whole Earth Review,* Fall 1991, pp. 84-86.

## COMPREHENSION

Answer these questions without looking back at the reading.

1. Where did this interview take place?
   **a.** Korea
   **b.** Japan
   **c.** Lhasa
   **d.** the U.S.
2. What religion did the Pashu Lama practice?
   **a.** Shinto
   **b.** Buddhism
   **c.** Christianity
   **d.** Islam
3. One important belief of this religion is:
   **a.** compassion
   **b.** vengeance
   **c.** redemption
   **d.** forgiveness
4. The doctrine of nonviolence was followed by
   **a.** George Bush;
   **b.** Mahatma Gandhi;
   **c.** Margaret Thatcher;
   **d.** Benazir Bhutto.
5. Which of the following is NOT a component of Tibetan Buddhism?
   **a.** meditation
   **b.** Karma
   **c.** reincarnation
   **d.** prayer

## ANALYSIS

Discuss the following questions with your class.

1. Summarize the hardships the Pashu Lama has endured. What was his reaction to these hardships?
2. The author writes, "Without a sign of rancor he points to the manacle scars on his wrists." What is meant by "without a sign of rancor"? Would you react in the same way? Why or why not?
3. This story deals with the clash between governments and religion. What is the relationship between government and religion is in the U.S.? Explain.
4. What is the relationship between government and religion in your own country? Explain it to your class.

### Threads

The Baha'i religion, founded in Iran in 1844, teaches that each prophet-founder of the world's religions revealed the will of God for a particular time and place in history.

## VOCABULARY

There are several places in this reading where the author uses an unfamiliar word, along with its definition. Find those places and list the words and their definitions here.

_____

_____

_____

_____

*IT WORKS!*
*Learning Strategy:*
*Vocabulary Focus*

At right: A Baptist congregation on Sunday morning where a rich tradition of singing and testifying continues. Far right: A Roman Catholic Cathedral.

## PREREADING ACTIVITY

Can you think of any traditional stories that are told in your culture to teach a lesson in morality? First, write the story in your journal. Then, share the story with a classmate, preferably one from another culture.

## Threads

Major American churches:
Roman Catholic 26.2%
Baptist 19.4%
Methodist 8%
Lutheran 5.2%

# CRAIGAVON BRIDGE[1]

## Seamus Deane

Father Regan was lighting a candle in his dark classroom at the foot of the statue of the Blessed Virgin[2]. Regan permitted no overhead lights when he gave his formal religious address at the beginning of our last year in school. Regan was small, neat, economical. After he said "Boys," he stopped for a bit and looked at us. Then he dropped his eyes and kept them down until he said, more loudly this time, "Boys." He had complete silence this time.

"Some of you here, one or two of you perhaps, know the man I am going to talk about today. You may not know you know him, but that doesn't matter.

"More than thirty years ago, during the troubles in Derry, this man was arrested and charged with the murder of a policeman. The policeman had been walking home one night over Craigavon Bridge. It was a bleak night, November, nineteen hundred and twenty-two. The time was two in the morning. The policeman was off duty; he was wearing civilian clothes. There were two men coming the other way, on the other side of the bridge. As the policeman neared the middle of the bridge, these two men crossed over to his side. They were strolling, talking casually. They had their hats pulled down over their faces and their coat collars turned up for it was wet and cold. As they passed the policeman, one of them said "Goodnight" and the policeman returned the greeting. And then suddenly he found himself grabbed from behind and lifted off his feet. He tried to kick but one of the men held his legs. "This is for Neil McLaughlin," said one. "May you rot in the hell you're going to, you murdering bastard." They lifted him to the parapet[3] and held him there for a minute like a log and let him stare down at the water—seventy, eighty feet below. Then they pushed him over and he fell, with the street lights shining on his wet coat until he disappeared into the shadows with a splash. They heard him thrashing and he shouted once. Then he went under. His body was washed up three days later. No one saw them. They went home and they said nothing.

"A week later a man was arrested and charged with the murder. He was brought to trial. But the only evidence the police had was that he was the friend and workmate of Neil McLaughlin, who had been murdered by a policeman a month before. The story was that, before McLaughlin died on the street where he had been shot, coming out of the newspaper office where he worked, he had whispered the name of the killer to this man who had been arrested. And this man had been heard to swear revenge, to get the policeman—let's call him Mahon—in revenge for his friend's death. There was no point in going to the law, of course; justice would never be done; everyone knew that, especially in those years. So maybe the police thought they could beat an admission out of him, but he did not flinch from his story. That night he was not even in the city. He had been sent by his newspaper to Letterkenny twenty miles away, and he had several witnesses to prove it. The case was thrown out. People were surprised, even though they believed the man to be innocent. Innocence was no guarantee for a Catholic then. Nor is it now.

"Well I wasn't even in the city in those days. But I met this man several times and we became friendly. I was then a young curate[4] and this man was prominent in local sporting circles and he helped in various ways to raise money for the parish[5] building fund. One night, in the sacristy[6] of the Long Tower Church, just down the road from here, he told me that he had not been to confession in twenty years. He had something on his conscience that no penance could relieve. I told him to trust in God's infinite mercy; I offered to hear his confession; I offered to find someone else, a monk I knew down in Portglenone, to whom he could go, in case he did not want to confess to me. But no, he wouldn't go. No penance, he said, would be any use, because, in his heart, he could not feel sorrow for what he had done. But he wanted to tell someone, not as a confession, but in confidence.

"So he told me about being arrested. He told me about the beatings he had been given—rubber truncheons[7], punches, kicks, threats to put him over the bridge. He told me how he had resisted these assaults and never wavered.

"Oh," said I, "that's just a testimony to the strength you get from knowing you are in the right."

"He looked at me in amazement. 'D 'ye think that's what I wanted to tell you? The story of my innocence? For God's sake, Father, can't you see? I wasn't innocent. I was guilty. I killed Mahon and I'd kill him again if he came through that door this minute. That's why I can't confess. I have no sorrow, nor resolve not to do it again. No pity. Mahon shot my best friend dead in the street, for nothing. He was a drunken policeman with a gun, looking for a Teague to kill, and he left that man's wife with two young children and would have got off scot-free for the rest of his days, probably promoted for sterling service. And Neil told me as he lay there, with the blood draining from him, that Mahon did it. "Billy Mahon, Billy Mahon the policeman," that's what he said. And even then, I had to run back into the doorway and leave his body there in the street because they started shooting down the street from the city walls. And I'm not sorry I got Mahon and I told him what it was for before I threw him over that bridge and he knew, just too late, who I was when I said "Goodnight" to him. It was goodnight all right. One murdering bastard less.'

"Boys, that man went to the grave without confessing that sin. And think of all the wrongs that were done in that incident. Two men were murdered. Two men—three, for there was another man whose name was never mentioned—were murderers. Indeed maybe there was another murderer, for it's possible that Mahon was not the policeman involved. And there were perjurers who swore that the accused was elsewhere that night. And there were policemen who assaulted a man in custody. And there were judges who would certainly have acquitted any policeman, no matter how guilty, and would have found guilty any Catholic, no matter how innocent, on the slightest shred of evidence. The whole situation makes men evil. Evil men make the whole situation. And these days, similar things occur. Some of you boys may feel like getting involved when you leave school, because you sincerely believe that you would be on the side of justice, fighting for the truth. But, boys, let me tell you, there is a judge who sees all, knows all and is never unjust; there is a judge whose punishments and rewards are beyond the range of human imagining; there is a Law greater than the laws of human justice, far greater than the law of revenge, more enduring than the laws of any state whatsoever. That Judge is God, and Law is God's Law and the issue at stake is your immortal soul.

"We live, boys, in a world that will pass away. The shadows that candle throws upon the walls of this room are as substantial as we. Injustice, tyranny, freedom, national independence are realities that will fade too for they are not ultimate realities and the only life worth living is a life lived in the light of the ultimate. I know there are some who believe that the poor man who committed that murder was justified, and that he will be forgiven by an all-merciful God for what he did. That may be. I fervently hope that it is so, for who would judge God's mercy? But it is true too of the policeman; he may have been as plagued by guilt as his own murderer; he may have justified himself too; he may have refused sorrow and known no peace of mind; he may have forgiven himself or he may have been forgiven by God. It is not for us to judge. But it is for us to distinguish, to see the difference between wrong done to us and equal wrong done by us; to know that our transient life, no matter how scarred, how broken, how miserable it may be, is also God's miracle and gift; that we may not destroy it. If we destroy it in another, we destroy it in ourselves. Boys, as you enter upon your last year with us, you are on the brink of entering a world of wrong, insult, injury, unemployment, a world where the unjust hold power and the ignorant rule. But there is an inner peace nothing can reach; no insult can violate, no corruption can deprave. Hold to that; it is what your childish innocence once was and what your adult maturity must become. Hold to that. I bless you all."

And he raised his hand and made the sign of the Cross above our heads and crossed the room, blew out the candle as the bell rang wildly in the chapel tower and asked that the light be switched on. He left in silence with the candle smoking heavily behind him at the foot of the statute, stubby in its thick drapery of wax.

"That was your grandfather," said McShane to me. "I know that story too."

I derided him. I had heard the story too, but I wasn't going to take it on before everyone else. Anyway, it was just folklore. I had heard it when I was much younger and lay on the landing at night listening to the grown-ups talking in the kitchen below and had leaned over the banisters and imagined it was the edge of the parapet and that I was falling, falling down to the river of the hallway, as deaf and shining as a log.

[1] This story takes place in Northern Ireland, site of "The Troubles," or the fight between Protestants and Catholics, as well as the fight for independence from England.

[2] A reference to the Virgin Mary, the mother of Jesus.

[3] Low wall or railing.

[4] An assistant to a clergyman.

[5] A territory under the charge of a priest.

[6] A room in a church for holding sacred objects.

[7] Clubs.

Source: *Granta* 37, Autumn 1991, pp. 177-184.

## COMPREHENSION

Answer these questions without looking back at the story. Answer the questions true or false.

_____ **1.** This story takes place in Northern Ireland.

_____ **2.** The priest told this story on the first day of school.

_____ **3.** The policeman was shot because he had killed another man.

_____ **4.** McLaughlin was found guilty of the murder of the policeman, Bill Mahon.

_____ **5.** McLaughlin was beaten by the police when he was in custody.

_____ **6.** Several witnesses lied about McLaughlin's activities on the night of the murder.

_____ **7.** McLaughlin confessed to the murder to the police.

_____ **8.** McLaughlin was sorry he killed Billy Mahon.

## ANALYSIS

confession          revenge          perjurer
penance             innocent         conscience

Using the vocabulary items above, which are taken from the reading, write six discussion questions based on this reading. Ask your questions in a small group of classmates.

**1.** _____
_____
_____

**2.** _____
_____
_____

**3.** _____
_____
_____

**4.** _____
_____
_____

**5.** _____
_____
_____

## Threads

There are 31.5 million Muslims in the former USSR.

6. _____

_____

_____

## GRAMMAR

1. In the following exercise, you will reread some of the priest's words to his students. Try to paraphrase them in your own words.

   a. There is a judge who sees all, knows all and is never unjust; there is a judge whose punishments and rewards are beyond the range of human imagining; there is a Law greater than the laws of human justice, far greater than the law of revenge, more enduring than the laws of any state whatsoever.

   _____

   _____

   _____

   b. The shadows that candle throws upon the walls of this room are as substantial as we.

   _____

   _____

   c. Injustice, tyranny, freedom, national independence are realities that will fade too far for they are not ultimate realities and the only life worth living is a life lived in the light of the ultimate.

   _____

   _____

   _____

   _____

## Threads

We have just enough religion to make us hate, but not enough to make us love one another.

Johnathan Swift
1667-1745

   d. It is for us to distinguish, to see the difference between wrong done to us and equal wrong done by us; to know that our transient life, no matter how scarred, how broken, how miserable it may be, is also God's miracle and gift; that we may not destroy it.

   _____

   _____

   _____

   _____

## Themes

### DISCUSS

*IT WORKS!*
*Learning Strategy:*
*Note Taking*

What are the major religions found in your country? Choose one that you are familiar with and describe it for your classmates. During the discussion, make notes of the important features of each of the religions discussed. Use a separate notecard for each religion covered. Then, write a question asking something you would like to know more about regarding one of the religions your classmates described.

### DEBATE AND ROLE-PLAY

Imagine that you, with four other people, have been chosen to help plan a newly formed community. You have funding only for one religion's place of worship, however.

Which religion shall have the building? Play the role of a person advocating a particular religion's claim in that community. There is one restriction, however: you cannot be an advocate for your own religion. (That is, if you are a Catholic, you must argue that some *other* religion deserves the building).

### WRITE

Choose one of the topics below to write about.

**A.** Has religion played an important part in your life (either by its absence or its presence)? Write a description of the role it has had in your life.
**B.** "Craigavon Bridge" and "Pashu Lama" both deal with religious persecution. However, the reaction to persecution is different in these two readings. What were the reactions to persecution in the cases of Catholicism and Buddhism?

## The Cultural Dimension

1. Interview a classmate about an important religious symbol he or she is familiar with (for example, the cross in Christianity). Ask him or her to draw the symbol and explain its significance. Take notes or tape record your interview.
2. Interview someone outside your class about his or her opinion of the role of religion in the U.S.* Prepare at least five questions about this topic.

---

*Many Americans consider the discussion of religion to be impolite, since it deals with a "personal" subject. When you conduct this interview, be sure you make it clear why you are asking, and do not be offended if someone refuses to answer your questions.

Tape record your interview or take detailed notes. Write a report on the results of your interview.

3. Write two questions that you would like to add to this chapter. Ask your classmates your questions.

## Self-Evaluation Questionnaire

Make a list of new things you learned from this chapter.

1. _____
2. _____
3. _____
4. _____
5. _____
6. _____
7. _____
8. _____
9. _____
10. _____

As you did in previous chapters, think about the goals you set at the beginning of the chapter. How well did you perform? Review your progress, then rate yourself on how you think you did in each of the following areas for this chapter. Give yourself the following ratings:

**5 excellent  4 good  3 average  2 fair  1 poor**

| | RATING |
|---|---|
| **A.** Improved reading speed | _____ |
| **B.** Understood main ideas | _____ |
| **C.** Increased vocabulary understanding | _____ |
| **D.** Learned more about the topic of the chapter | _____ |
| **E.** Developed more understanding of style and grammar | _____ |

Compare your ratings with the objectives you set on the first page of this chapter.

# Language

# PLANNING & GOALS

List in order of priority (with 1 as the 'most important') the objectives that are important to you in this chapter.

*IT WORKS!*
*Learning Strategy:*
*Setting Goals*

| GOAL | RANK |
|------|------|
| **A.** To increase reading speed | _____ |
| **B.** To increase comprehension of main ideas | _____ |
| **C.** To improve vocabulary understanding | _____ |
| **D.** To learn more about the information in this chapter | _____ |
| **E.** To improve understanding of style and grammar | _____ |

# LOOKING AHEAD

Although you have been focusing on language indirectly throughout this book, this chapter will discuss language directly. Language is central in the lives of humans—they go to war over it, find comfort in it, record history with it, and use it to survive. Yet, language is a great mystery in many ways. It is both easy and difficult to learn, and it seems we never finish learning it.

The following readings on language are included in this chapter:

"Iron and Silk," by Mark Salzman

"Seventeen Syllables," by Hisaye Yamamoto

"You Are What You Say," by Robin Lakoff

"Cherry Tree," by Natalie Merchant

1. Which of these titles interests you most?
2. Which title(s) makes it difficult to predict the subject matter of the reading? Look ahead briefly at those readings and determine what they are about.
3. Do you find it difficult to understand the lyrics of songs when you hear them on the radio?

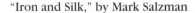

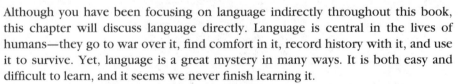

*LEARNING STRATEGY*

**Managing Your Learning: Thinking about a topic before reading about it helps you to prepare for your reading assignments.**

Sometimes you know more about a subject than you realize. Below you will find ten words associated with language. On the line next to each word, write the *first thing* that comes to your mind in association with this word. Compare your associations with a partner.

**a.** English _____

**b.** grammar _____

**c.** vocabulary _____

**d.** dictionary _____

**e.** words _____

**f.** books _____

**g.** writing _____

**h.** speaking _____

**i.** listening _____

**j.** pronunciation _____

Were there any words that you and your partner responded to in exactly the same way? Why do you think that happened? Which ones did you respond to completely differently?

## Try a New Strategy

Realizing how much you have learned can be very encouraging. Think about everything you have learned in the last few weeks about the English language. Make a list of these things—include new idioms, strategies, facts, processes. Be proud of your accomplishments!

Gary Larson © 1985
Universal Press Syndicate

## LEARNING STRATEGY

**Understanding and Using Emotion: Humor helps you to relax, which in turn helps you feel good about language learning.**

**Beginning duck**

## LISTENING

Create your own listening lesson. Work with a partner or small group and decide what type of listening material you would like to use. It could be a video, a television or radio program, a song, or anything else you find. Create a presentation of what you chose.

## PREREADING QUESTION

Do you remember your first English teacher? Write a description of him or her in your journal. Share your description with a partner.

# IRON AND SILK[1]

*Mark Salzman*

I'd been interested in China since I was thirteen. I had seen the television movie *Kung Fu* and decided right away that peace of mind and a shaved head were what I had always wanted. My parents supported by interest, buying all sorts of books about kung fu and Chinese art for me; they even enrolled me in a kung fu school, although they did not let me shave my head. I practiced several hours a day, tried to overcome pain by walking to school barefoot in the snow, and let my kung fu teacher pound me senseless in cemeteries at night so that I might learn to "die well." I enjoyed all of this so much that my interest continued through high school, and spread to wanting to learn Chinese painting and calligraphy[2] and then the language itself.

I went to Yale and majored in Chinese literature. By the time I finished college, I was fluent in Mandarin and nearly so in Cantonese[3], had struggled through a fair amount of classical Chinese and had translated the works of a modern poet. Oddly, though, I had no desire to go to China; it sounded like a giant penal colony to me, and besides, I have never liked traveling much. I did need a job, though, so I applied to and was accepted by the Yale-China Association to teach English at Hunan Medical College in Changsha from August 1982 to July 1984.

The college assigned three classes to me: twenty-six doctors and teachers of medicine, four men and one woman identified as "the Middle-Aged English Teachers," and twenty-five medical students ranging in age from twenty-two to twenty-eight. First I met the doctors, who stood up to applaud my entrance into the classroom and remained standing while the Class Monitor read a prepared statement that welcomed and praised me.

Their English ability ranged form nearly fluent to practically hopeless. At the end of the first week of classes the Class Monitor read aloud the results of their "Suggestions for Better Study" meeting: "Dear Teacher Mark. You are an active boy! Your lessons are very humorous and very wonderful. To improve our class, may we suggest that in the future we (1) spend more time reading, (2) spend more time listening, (3) spend more time writing and (4) spend more time speaking. Also some students feel you are moving too quickly through the book. However, some students request that you speed up a little, because the material is too elementary. We hope we can struggle together to overcome these contradictions! Thank you, our dear teacher."

I was next introduced to the medical students, whom I taught only once a week, on Tuesday nights. They were nearly faint with excitement over meeting a foreign teacher; when I first walked into the room they didn't move or breathe, and no one dared look directly at me. The Monitor yelled, "Stand up!" and they rose with such formality that I did not know how to respond. At last I saluted them gravely and yelled in Chinese, "Sit down!" They looked stunned, then exploded into cheers, giving me the thumbs-up sign[4] and speaking to me all at once in Chinese. It seemed that the tension had been released, so when they calmed down I asked them to introduce themselves in English. At first they giggled and whispered to one another, then slowly they lowered their heads, turned pale and went mute.

---

[1] This reading was taken from a book of the same name. It has been made into a film, which you may want to look for in your local video store.

[2] The art of beautiful writing, done usually with special pens or brushes.

[3] Mandarin and Cantonese are Chinese languages

[4] The thumbs-up sign is a gesture meaning that someone has done something well, or that the gesturer approves of something

Source: *Iron and Silk,* New York: Random House, 1986, 17–19.

## COMPREHENSION

Answer these questions without looking back at the reading.

1. What caused the author to become interested in China?
   a. visiting with his parents
   b. seeing the movie *Kung Fu*
   c. shaving his head
   d. seeing Chinese art
2. Why didn't the author initially want to go to China?
   a. He couldn't speak Chinese.
   b. He couldn't get a job.
   c. He didn't like traveling.
   d. His parents wouldn't allow it.
3. The majority of the author's students were
   a. doctors or medical students
   b. English teachers
   c. kung fu students
   d. poets

## ANALYSIS

Discuss the following questions in a small group.

1. When the Monitor yelled, "Stand up!" to the students in the class, why do you think Mr. Salzman then yelled at them to "Sit down!"? Why were they amused by this?
2. What do you think about the students' "suggestions" for improving their studies? How do you think the teacher felt about them?
3. When did you become interested in traveling to an English-speaking country? Do you remember how you became interested?

## PREREADING QUESTION

What is haiku? Look in the library or ask a classmate for an example of haiku. Share it with the class.

# SEVENTEEN SYLLABLES

*Hisaye Yamamoto[1]*

The first Rosie knew that her mother had taken to writing poems was one evening when she finished one and read it aloud for her daughter's approval. It was about cats, and Rosie pretended to understand it thoroughly and appreciate it no end, partly because she hesitated to disillusion her mother about the quantity and quality of Japanese she had learned in all the years now that she had been going to Japanese school every Saturday (and Wednesday, too, in the summer). Even so, her mother must have been skeptical about the depth of Rosie's understanding, because she explained afterwards about the kind of poem she was trying to write.

See, Rosie, she said, it was a *haiku,* a poem in which she must pack all her meaning into seventeen syllables only, which were divided into three lines of five, seven, and five syllables. In the one she had just read, she had tried to capture the charm of a kitten, as well as comment on the superstition that owning a cat of three colors meant good luck.

"Yes, yes, I understand. How utterly lovely," Rosie said, and her mother, either satisfied or seeing through the deception and resigned, went back to composing.

The truth was that Rosie was lazy; English lay ready on the tongue but Japanese had to be searched for and examined, and even then put forth tentatively (probably to meet with laughter). It was so much easier to say yes, yes, even when one meant no, no. Besides, this was what was in her mind to say: I was looking through one of your magazines from Japan last night, Mother, and towards the back I found some *haiku* in English that delighted me. There was one that made me giggle off and on until I fell asleep—

> *It is morning, and lo!*
> *I lie awake, comme il faut,[2]*
> *sighing for some dough.*

Now, how to reach her mother, how to communicate the melancholy song? Rosie knew formal Japanese by fits and starts, her mother had even less English, no French. It was much more possible to say yes, yes.

It developed that her mother was writing the *haiku* for a daily newspaper, the *Mainichi Shimbun,* that was published in San Francisco. Los Angeles, to be sure, was closer to the farming community in which the Hayashi family lived and several Japanese vernaculars were printed there, but Rosie's parents said they preferred the tone of the northern paper. Once a week, the *Mainichi* would have a section devoted to *haiku,* and her mother became an extravagant contributor, taking for herself the blossoming pen name, Ume Hanazono.

So Rosie and her father lived for awhile with two women, her mother and Ume Hanazono. Her mother (Tome Hayashi by name) kept house, cooked, washed, and, along with her husband and the Carrascos, the Mexican family hired for the harvest, did her ample share of picking tomatoes out in the sweltering fields and boxing them in tidy strata[3] in the cool packing shed. Ume Hanazono, who came to life after the dinner dishes were done, was an earnest, muttering stranger who often neglected speaking when spoken to and stayed busy at the parlor table as late as midnight scribbling with pencil on scratch paper or carefully copying characters on good paper with her fat, pale green Parker.[4]

The new interest had some repercussions on the household routine. Before, Rosie had been accustomed to her parents and herself taking their hot baths early and going to bed almost immediately afterwards, unless her parents challenged each other to a game of flower cards or unless company dropped in. Now if her father wanted to play cards, he had to resort to solitaire (at which he always cheated fearlessly), and if a group of friends came over, it was bound to contain someone who was also writing haiku, and the small assemblage would be split in two, her father entertaining the non-literary members and her mother comparing ecstatic notes with the visiting poet.

If they went out, it was more of the same thing. But Ume Hanazono's life span, even for a poet's, was very brief—perhaps three months at most.

[1] Hisaye Yamamoto was born in Redondo Beach, California. She was interned in a relocation camp in Poston, Arizona, from 1942 to 1945. She currently lives in Southern California.

[2] Translation: 'As it should be.'

[3] Layers or levels (singular is 'stratum').

[4] Parker is the brand name of a type of pen.

Source: Excerpt from *Seventeen Syllables and Other Stories*, 1988. Latham, New York: Kitchen Table: Women of Color Press; pp. 8–19.

## COMPREHENSION

Answer these questions true or false, without looking back at the story.

_____ 1. Rosie is Japanese-American.

_____ 2. Rosie speaks Japanese fluently.

_____ 3. Rosie's mother wrote a poem about a kitten.

_____ 4. Rosie communicated easily with her mother.

_____ 5. The Hayashi family are farmworkers.

_____ 6. Ume Hanazono and Tome Hayashi are the same person.

_____ 7. Rosie's mother wrote poetry for the local English newspaper.

_____ 8. The Hayashis live in California.

## ANALYSIS

*IT WORKS!*
*Learning Strategy:*
*Analyzing*

In this exercise, you will be asked to *draw inferences* about the story. That is, you will "read beyond" the story, and decide what the feelings or motivations of the characters are. Look at the following statements taken from the story, then answer the questions that follow it. Work with a partner.

1. "It was about cats, and Rosie pretended to understand it thoroughly and appreciate it no end, partly because she hesitated to disillusion her mother about the quantity and quality of Japanese she had learned in all the years now that she had been going to Japanese school every Saturday (and Wednesday, too, in the summer)."

   How good do you think Rosie's knowledge of Japanese is?

2. "'Yes, yes, I understand. How utterly lovely,' Rosie said, and her mother, either satisfied or seeing through the deception and resigned, went back to composing."

   How sincere is Rosie in her reaction to her mother's poem?

3. "Now if her father wanted to play cards, he had to resort to solitaire (at which he always cheated fearlessly), and if a group of friends came over, it was bound to contain someone who was also writing *haiku,* and the small assemblage would be split in two, her father entertaining the non-literary members and her mother comparing ecstatic notes with the visiting poet."

   How do you think Rosie's father feels about his wife's writing career?

4. "But Ume Hanazono's life span, even for a poet's, was very brief—perhaps three months at most."

   Why do you think Rosie's mother stopped writing after only three months?

## PREREADING QUESTION

Do you think there is a difference between men and women in the way they speak English? What about the way they speak your first language? Discuss these questions with your class.

# YOU ARE WHAT YOU SAY[1]

## Robin Lakoff[2]

"Women's language" is that pleasant (dainty?), euphemistic[3], never-aggressive way of talking we learned as little girls. Cultural bias was built into the language we were allowed to speak, the subjects we were allowed to speak about, and the ways we were spoken of. Having learned our linguistic lesson well, we go out in the world, only to discover that we are communicative cripples—damned if we do, and damned if we don't.

If we refuse to talk "like a lady," we are ridiculed and criticized for being unfeminine. ("She thinks like a man" is, at best, a left-handed compliment.) If we do learn all the fuzzy-headed, unassertive language of our sex, we are ridiculed for being unable to think clearly, unable to take part in a serious discussion, and therefore unfit to hold a position of power.

It doesn't take much of this for a woman to begin feeling she deserves such treatment because of inadequacies in her own intelligence and education.

"Women's language" shows up in all levels of English. For example, women are encouraged and allowed to make far more precise discriminations in naming colors than men do. Words like *mauve, beige, ecru, aquamarine, lavender,* and so on, are unremarkable in a woman's active vocabulary, but largely absent from that of most men. I know of no evidence suggesting that women actually *see* a wider range of colors than men do. It is simply that fine discriminations of this sort are relevant to women's vocabularies, but not to men's; to men, who control most of the interesting affairs of the world, such distinctions are trivial—irrelevant.

In the area of syntax, we find similar gender-related peculiarities of speech. There is one construction, in particular, that women use conversationally far more than men: the tag-question. A tag is midway between an outright statement and a yes-no question; it is less assertive than the former, but more confident than the later.

A *flat statement* indicates confidence in the speaker's knowledge and is fairly certain to be believed; a *question* indicates a lack of knowledge on some point and implies that the gap in the speaker's knowledge can and will be remedied by an answer. For example, if, at a Little League[4] game, I have had my glasses off, I can legitimately ask someone else: "Was the player out at third?" A *tag question*, being intermediate between statement and question, is used when the speaker is stating a claim, but lacks full confidence in the truth of that claim. So if I say, "Is Joan here?" I will probably not be surprised if my respondent answers "no"; but if I say, "Joan is here, isn't she?" instead, chances are I am already biased in favor of a positive answer, wanting only confirmation. I still want a response, but I have enough knowledge (or think I have) to predict that response. A tag question, then, might be thought of as a statement that doesn't demand to be believed by anyone but the speaker, a way of giving leeway, of not forcing the addressee to go along with the views of the speaker.

Another common use of the tag question is in small talk when the speaker is trying to elicit conversation: "Sure is hot here, isn't it?"

But in discussing personal feelings or opinions, only the speaker normally has any way of knowing the correct answer. Sentences such as "I have a headache, don't I?" are clearly ridiculous. But there are other examples where it is the speaker's opinions, rather than perceptions, for which corroboration is sought, as in "The situation in Southeast Asia is terrible, isn't it?"

While there are, of course, other possible interpretations of a sentence like this, one possibility is that the speaker has a particular answer in mind—"yes" or "no"—but is reluctant to state it baldly. This sort of tag question is more apt to be used by women than by men in conversation. Why is this the case?

The tag question allows a speaker to avoid commitment, and thereby avoid conflict with the addressee. The problem is that, by so doing, speakers may also give the impression of not really being sure of themselves, or looking to the addressee for confirmation of their views. This uncertainty is reinforced in more subliminal ways, too. There is a peculiar sentence intonation-pattern, used almost exclusively by women, as far as I know, which changes a declarative answer into a question. The effect of using the rising inflection typical of a yes-no question is to imply that the speaker is seeking confirmation, even though the speaker is clearly the only one who has the requisite information, which is why the question was put to her in the first place:

(Q) When will dinner be ready?

(A) Oh . . . around six o'clock . . . ?

It is as though the second speaker were saying, "Six o'clock—if that's okay with you, if you agree." The person being addressed is put in the position of having to provide confirmation. One likely consequence of this sort of speech-pattern in a woman is that, often unbeknownst to herself, the speaker builds a reputation of tentativeness, and others will refrain from taking her seriously or trusting her with any real responsibilities, since she "can't make up her mind," and "isn't sure of herself."

Such idiosyncrasies may explain why women's language sounds more "polite" than men's. It is polite to leave a decision open, not impose your mind, your views, or claims on anyone else. So a tag question is a kind of polite statement, in that it does not force agreement or belief on the addressee. In the same way a request is a polite command, in that it does not force obedience on the addressee, but rather suggests something be done as a favor to the speaker. A clearly stated order implies a threat of certain consequences if it is not followed, and— even more polite—implies that the speaker is in a superior position and able to enforce the order. By couching wishes in the form of a request, on the other hand, a speaker implies that if the request is not carried out, only the speaker will suffer; noncompliance cannot harm the addressee. So the decision is really left up to the addressee. The distinction becomes clear in these examples:

Close the door.

Please close the door.

Will you close the door.

Will you please close the door?

Won't you close the door?

In the same ways as words and speech patterns used *by* women undermine her image, those used to *describe* women make matters even worse. Often a word may be used of both men and women (and perhaps of things as well); but when it is applied to women, it assumes a special meaning that, by implication rather than outright assertion, is derogatory to women as a group.

The use of euphemisms has this effect. A euphemism is a substitute for a word that has acquired a bad connotation by association with something unpleasant or embarrassing. But almost as soon as the new word comes into common usage, it takes on the same old bad connotations, since feelings about the things or people referred to are not altered by a change of name; thus new euphemisms must be constantly found.

There is one euphemism for *woman* still very much alive. The word, of course, is *lady*. *Lady* has a masculine counterpart, namely *gentleman*, occasionally shortened to *gent*. But for some reason *lady* is very much commoner than *gent(leman)*.

The decision to use *lady* rather than *woman*, or vice versa, may considerably alter the sense of a sentence, as the following examples show:

**(a)** A woman (lady) I know is a dean at Berkeley.

**(b)** A woman (lady) I know makes amazing things out of shoelaces and old boxes.

The use of *lady* in (a) imparts a frivolous, or nonserious, tone to the sentence: the matter under discussion is not one of great moment. Similarly, in (b), using *lady* here would suggest that the speaker considered the "amazing things" not to be serious art, but merely a hobby or an aberration. If *woman* is used, she might be a serious sculptor. To say *lady doctor* is very condescending, since no one ever says *gentleman doctor* or even *man doctor*. For example, mention in the San Francisco *Chronicle* of January 31, 1972, of Madalyn Murray O'Hair as the *lady atheist* is scarcely defensible: sex is irrelevant to her philosophical position.

Many women argue that, on the other hand, *lady* carries with it overtones recalling the age of chivalry: conferring exalted stature on the person so referred to. This makes the term seem polite at first, but we must also remember that these implications are perilous: they suggest that a "lady" is helpless, and cannot do things by herself.

*Lady* can also be used to infer frivolousness, as in titles of organizations. Those that have a serious purpose (not merely that of enabling "the ladies" to spend time with one another) cannot use the word *lady* in their titles, but less serious ones may. Compare the *Ladies' Auxiliary* of a men's group, or the *Thursday Evening Ladies' Browning and Garden Society* with *Ladies' Liberation* or *Ladies' Strike for Peace*.

What is curious about this split is that *lady* is in origin a euphemism—a substitute that puts a better face on something people find uncomfortable—for *woman*. What kind of euphemism is it that subtly denigrates the people to whom it refers? Perhaps *lady* functions as a euphemism for *woman* because it does not contain the sexual implications present in *woman*: It is not "embarrassing" in that way. If this is so, we may expect that, in the future, *lady* will replace woman as the primary word for the human female, since *woman* will have become too blatantly sexual. That this distinction is already made in some contexts as least is shown in the following examples, where you can try replacing *woman* with *lady*:

**(a)** She's only twelve, but she's already a woman.

**(b)** After ten years in jail, Harry wanted to find a woman.

**(c)** She's my woman, see, so don't mess around with her.

Another common substitute for *woman* is *girl*. One seldom hears a man past the age of adolescence referred to as a boy, save in expressions like "going out with the boys," which are meant to suggest an air of adolescent frivolity and irresponsibility. But women of all ages are "girls": one can have a man—not a boy—Friday, but only a girl—never a woman or even a lady—Friday; women have girlfriends, but men do not—in a nonsexual sense—have boyfriends. It may be that this use of *girl* is euphemistic in the same way the use of *lady* is: in stressing the idea of immaturity, it removes the sexual connotations lurking in *woman*. *Girl* brings to mind irresponsibility: you don't send a girl to do a woman's errand (or even, for that matter, a boy's errand). She is a person who is both too immature and too far from real life to be entrusted with responsibilities or with decisions of any serious or important nature.

Now let's take a pair of words which, in terms of the possible relationships in an earlier society, where simple male-female equivalents, analogous to *bull: cow*. Suppose we find that, for independent reasons, society has changed in a such a way that the original meanings now are irrelevant. Yet the words have not been discarded, but have acquired new meanings, metaphorically related to their original senses. But suppose these new metaphorical uses are no longer parallel to each other. By seeing where the parallelism breaks down, we discover something about the different roles played by men and women in this culture. One good example of such a divergence through time is found in the pair, *master: mistress.* Once used with reference to one's power over servants, these words have become unusable today in their original master-servant sense as the relationship has become less prevalent in our society. But the words are still common.

Unless used with reference to animals, *master* now generally refers to a man who has acquired consummate[5] ability in some field, normally nonsexual. But its feminine counterpart cannot be used this way. It is practically restricted to its sexual sense of "paramour." We start out with two terms, both roughly paraphrasable as "one who has power over another." But the masculine form, once one person is no longer able to have absolute power over another, becomes usable metaphorically in the sense of "having power over *something.*" *Master* requires as its object only the name of some activity, something inanimate and abstract. But *mistress* requires a masculine noun in the possessive to precede it. One cannot say: "Rhonda is a mistress." One must be *someone's* mistress. A man is defined by what he does, a woman by her sexuality, that is, in terms of one particular aspect of her relationship to men. It is one thing to be an *old master* like Hans Holbein, and another to be an *old mistress.*

The same is true of the words *spinster* and *bachelor*—gender words for "one who is not married." The resemblance ends with the definition. While *bachelor* is a neuter term, often used as a compliment, *spinster* normally is used pejoratively[6], with connotations of prissiness, fussiness, and so on. To be a bachelor implies that one has the choice of marrying or not, and this is what makes the idea of a bachelor existence attractive in the popular literature. He has been pursued and has successfully eluded his pursuers. But a spinster is one who has not been pursued, or at least not seriously. She is old, unwanted goods. The metaphorical connotations of *bachelor* generally suggests sexual freedom; of *spinster,* puritanism[7] or celibacy.

These examples could be multiplied. It is generally considered a *faux pas,* in society, to congratulate a woman on her engagement, while it is correct to congratulate her fiance. Why is this? The reason seems to be that it is impolite to remind people of things that may be uncomfortable to them. To congratulate a woman on her engagement is really to say, "Thank goodness! You had a close call!" For the man, on the other hand, there is no such danger. His choosing to marry is viewed as a good thing, but not something essential.

The linguistic double standard holds throughout the life of the relationship. After marriage, bachelor and spinster become man and wife, not man and woman. The woman whose husband dies remains "John's widow"; John, however, is never "Mary's widower."

Finally, why is it that salesclerks and others are so quick to call women customers "dear," "honey," and other terms of endearment they really have no business using? A male customer would never put up with it. But women, like children, are supposed to enjoy these endearments, rather than being offended by them.

In more ways than one, it's time to speak up.

[1] This title is a play on the adage "You are what you eat."

[2] Robin Lakoff is a professor of linguistics at the University of California, Berkeley.

[3] A euphemism is a more pleasant way of saying something. One example is "sanitary engineer" instead of "garbage collector." Can you think of others?

[4] Organized baseball games for children.

[5] Most excellent.

[6] As an insult.

[7] Having very strict moral values, like the Puritans, a religious group in early American history.

Source: *Ms* Magazine, July, 1974.

## ANALYSIS

Discuss the following questions with a partner. Make notes of your answers, then discuss them with the class.

1. In the first paragraph, Lakoff uses the phrase "damned if we do, and damned if we don't." What does she mean?
2. In the second paragraph, the author uses the phrase "left-handed compliment." What is meant by the phrase "left-handed"?
3. The fifth through tenth paragraphs talk about *tag questions*. What is a tag question? Why are these characteristic of women's speech?
4. How does Lakoff consider women's speech more polite than men's? Does she think this is a "good" thing? Why or why not?
5. Discuss the difference between the words *spinster* and *bachelor,* and *master* and *mistress.* Were you aware of the difference in their meaning before?
6. The author states that women use a wider variety of color terms in English than men do. Is this true in your first language? What color terms would men not normally use?
7. In what ways does the author think the word "lady" is problematic?

*IT WORKS!*
*Learning Strategy:*
*Vocabulary Focus*

## VOCABULARY

Look at the following five words or phrases. If you do not know what they mean, look them up in a dictionary. Then, create phrases or sentences that are examples of each item.

1. euphemism

   a. _____

   _____

   b. _____

   _____

2. faux pas

   a. _____

   _____

   b. _____

   _____

3. metaphor

   a. _____

   _____

   b. _____

   _____

4. double standard

## Threads

**There are 65 alphabets in use worldwide.**

*Guinness Book 1992*

**a.** _____

_____

**b.** _____

_____

**5.** small talk

**a.** _____

_____

**b.** _____

_____

Share your answers with a group of three other students. Which examples from the group did you find most interesting? Why?

*IT WORKS!*
*Learning Strategy:*
*Discuss Your Feelings*

## PREREADING ACTIVITY

What is illiteracy? What role does reading play in your life? Can you imagine not being able to read? In your journal, describe what reading means to you. Share your thoughts with a classmate.

*LEARNING STRATEGY*

**Understanding and Using Emotions: Music reduces your anxiety, helps you relax, and increases your enjoyment of language learning.**

The following "poem" is actually words from a popular song. If you wish, find the recording, (from the album, "In My Tribe" by 10,000 Maniacs) and listen to it as you read the lyrics.

## Cherry Tree

Over your shoulder,
please don't mind me
if my eyes have fallen onto your magazine
for I've been watching and wondering
why your face is changing
with every line you read.
All those lines and circles,
to me, a mystery.
Eve pull down the apple
and give a taste to me.
If she could it would be wonderful,
but my pride is in the way.
I cannot read to save my life,
I'm so ashamed to say.
I live in silence,
afraid to speak of my life in darkness
because I cannot read.
For all those lines and circles,
to me a mystery.
Eve pull down the apple and give a taste to me.
If she could it would be wonderful.
Then I wouldn't need someone else's eyes
to see what's in front of me.
No one guiding me.
It makes me humble to be so green
at what every kid can do when he learns A to Z,
but all those lines and circles just frighten me
and I fear that I'll be trampled
if you don't reach for me.
Before I run I'll have to take a fall.
And when I pick myself up,
so slowly I'll devour every one of those books
in the Tower of Knowledge.

*Natalie Merchant*

Source: From the album *In My Tribe*, by 10,000 Maniacs. Reprinted by kind permission of Christian Burial Music.

## Threads

**The English language contains 490,000 words and 300,000 technical terms.**

*Guinness Book 1992*

## Themes

What books have had an influence on you? Make a list of their titles (translate them into English as best as you are able), and compare your list with a partner's. Discuss your list with your class. Recommend your favorite book to your classmates.

### DEBATE

What is the most important part of learning a second language (for example, grammar, culture, etc.)? State your opinion, and then form a team with others who have the same or similar opinions.

State your team's opinion in one sentence:

_____

What are the reasons you believe this? (Again, state each reason as a sentence.)

1. _____
2. _____
3. _____
4. _____
(Use an additional piece of paper if you need more space.)

Your team should present its argument to the class. Each team should get the same amount of time to make its presentation.

A scene from Shakespeare's *Hamlet*, in Laurence Olivier's screen version available on video.

### ROLE-PLAY

Imagine it is your first day in an English class you attended. Do you remember how you felt about being there? Were you nervous? Excited? What was the teacher like?

In a small group, one student should play the role of the teacher, the remainder the students. Act out a first day in English class.

### WRITE

You have had a lot of experience by now with English classes. Design what you think would be the perfect English class. Think about what elements of learning have been important to you—what kinds of classes, time spent in an English speaking country, etc. How is your plan different form your experience? Describe your plan in writing, and explain what types of activities or assignments you think would be helpful to you learning English better.

## The Cultural Dimension

1. Interview a classmate on his or her experience with learning English. Prepare at least five questions to ask about this topic. Report on your interview to the class.
2. Interview a native English speaker about his or her experience in learning a foreign language. Prepare at least five questions about this topic. Tape record your interview or take detailed notes. Write a report on the results of your interview.

## Self-Evaluation Questionnaire

Make a list of new things you learned from this chapter.

1. _____
2. _____
3. _____
4. _____
5. _____
6. _____
7. _____

8. _____

9. _____

10. _____

You will recall that at the beginning of the chapter, you were asked to determine your goals. Now, think about your performance. Rate yourself on how you did in each of the following ares for this chapter. Give yourself the following ratings:

**5 excellent  4 good  3 average  2 fair  1 poor**

| | RATING |
|---|---|
| **A.** Improved reading speed | _____ |
| **B.** Understood main ideas | _____ |
| **C.** Increased vocabulary understanding | _____ |
| **D.** Learned more about the topic of the chapter | _____ |
| **E.** Developed more understanding of style and grammar | _____ |

Compare your ratings with the objectives you set on the first page of this chapter.

**8.** _____

**9.** _____

**10.** _____

You will recall that at the beginning of the chapter, you were asked to determine your goals. Now, think about your performance. Rate yourself on how you did in each of the following ares for this chapter. Give yourself the following ratings:

**5 excellent   4 good   3 average   2 fair   1 poor**

**RATING**

**A.** Improved reading speed _____

**B.** Understood main ideas _____

**C.** Increased vocabulary understanding _____

**D.** Learned more about the topic of the chapter _____

**E.** Developed more understanding of style and grammar _____

Compare your ratings with the objectives you set on the first page of this chapter.

# *Appendices*

If you are interested in your reading speed, you may use the table below to keep a record of the reading times for this book. Remember that your reading speed will vary depending on a number of factors, such as:

- purpose of reading
- familiarity with the subject matter
- difficulty of material
- type of reading (for example, newspaper article, poem, etc.)

| NAME OF READING | DATE | SPEED | NOTES |
|---|---|---|---|
| | | | |
| | | | |
| | | | |
| | | | |
| | | | |
| | | | |
| | | | |
| | | | |
| | | | |
| | | | |
| | | | |
| | | | |
| | | | |
| | | | |
| | | | |
| | | | |
| | | | |
| | | | |
| | | | |

| NAME OF READING | DATE | SPEED | NOTES |
|---|---|---|---|
| | | | |
| | | | |
| | | | |
| | | | |
| | | | |
| | | | |
| | | | |
| | | | |
| | | | |
| | | | |
| | | | |
| | | | |
| | | | |
| | | | |
| | | | |

# APPENDIX B  RECOMMENDED READING

Reading a variety of materials, and longer works in particular, will help improve your reading fluency.

Below are some titles of books that are related to the topics presented in this textbook.

*IT WORKS!*
*Learning Strategy:*
*Practicing*

## Changing Political Systems

*The Unbearable Lightness of Being*  by Milan Kundera
*Typical American*  by Gish Jen

## Population and Immigration

*The Joy Luck Club*  by Amy Tan
*China Boy*  by Gus Lee
*Hunger of Memory*  by Richard Rodriguez

## Food and World Hunger

*The Jungle*  by Upton Sinclair
*The Grapes of Wrath*  by John Steinbeck

## War

*The Red Badge of Courage*  by Stephen Crane
*My Brother Sam is Dead*  by James Lincoln Collier and Christopher Collier

## Eco-Politics

*The Old Man and the Sea*  by Ernest Hemingway
*The Mosquito Coast*  by Paul Theroux

## Travel

*The Innocents Abroad*  by Mark Twain
*What Am I Doing Here?*  by Bruce Chatwin

## Space

*The Right Stuff*  by Tom Wolfe
*The Sirens of Titan*  by Kurt Vonnegut, Jr.

## Media

*Fahrenheit 451*  by Ray Bradbury
*Being There*  by Jerzy Kosinski

## Religion

*The Chocolate War*  by Robert Cormier
*Pageant*  by Kathryn Lasky
*The Chosen*  by Chaim Potok

## Language

*You Just Don't Understand*  by Deborah Tannen
*The Mother Tongue: English and How It Got That Way*  by Bill Bryson

Use the following spaces to record any new words that you would like to remember. Note their pronunciation, definition, and use them in a sentence in order to help you remember them better.

An example is given.

_____cockpit_____ , ( _kŏk´pit_ ) _____a space in an airplane_____

_____for the pilot and crew_____

Sentence: _____The pilot made an announcement from the cockpit._____

_____

_____ , ( _____ ) _____

_____

Sentence: _____

_____

_____ , ( _____ ) _____

_____

Sentence: _____

_____

_____ , ( _____ ) _____

_____

Sentence: _____

_____

_____ , ( _____ ) _____

_____

Sentence: _____

_____

_____ , ( _____ ) _____

_____

Sentence: _____

_____

_____ , ( ) _____

_____

Sentence: _____

_____

_____ , ( ) _____

_____

Sentence: _____

_____

_____ , ( ) _____

_____

Sentence: _____

_____

_____ , ( ) _____

_____

Sentence: _____

_____

_____ , ( ) _____

_____

Sentence: _____

_____

_____ , ( ) _____

_____

Sentence: _____

_____

_____ , ( ) _____

_____

Sentence: _____

_____

_____ , (      ) _____

_____

Sentence: _____

_____

_____ , (      ) _____

_____

Sentence: _____

_____

_____ , (      ) _____

_____

Sentence: _____

_____

_____ , (      ) _____

_____

Sentence: _____

_____

_____ , (      ) _____

_____

Sentence: _____

_____

_____ , (      ) _____

_____

Sentence: _____

_____

_____ , (      ) _____

_____

Sentence: _____

_____

_____ , (                    ) _____

_____

Sentence: _____

_____

_____ , (                    ) _____

_____

Sentence: _____

_____

_____ , (                    ) _____

_____

Sentence: _____

_____

_____ , (                    ) _____

_____

Sentence: _____

_____

_____ , (                    ) _____

_____

Sentence: _____

_____

_____ , (                    ) _____

_____

Sentence: _____

_____

_____ , (                 ) _____

_____

Sentence: _____

_____

_____ , (                 ) _____

_____

Sentence: _____

_____

_____ , (                 ) _____

_____

Sentence: _____

_____

_____ , (                 ) _____

_____

Sentence: _____

_____

_____ , (                 ) _____

_____

Sentence: _____

_____

_____ , (                 ) _____

_____

Sentence: _____

_____

_____ , (                 ) _____

_____

Sentence: _____

_____